·PLANS·AND·ELEVATiONS·
·OF·THE·
ANTiENT · KHANS · PALACE ·
·AT·
·BAKSHiSARAi·
AND·OTHER·BUiLDiNGS·
·iN·
·CRiM·TARTARY·
·M·DCC·XCViII·

*Towers of
Crim Tartary*

TOWERS OF CRIM TARTARY

ENGLISH AND SCOTTISH
ARCHITECTS AND CRAFTSMEN
IN THE CRIMEA, 1762–1853

C. E. B. BRETT

SHAUN TYAS
DONINGTON
2005

Typeset and designed from the disc of the author by the publisher

Published by

SHAUN TYAS
1 High Street
Donington
Lincolnshire
PE11 4TA

ISBN

1 900289 73 3

Frontispiece illustration:
the Alupka Palace, main entrance.
Photograph: Terence Reeves-Smyth.

End-papers illustration:
Bilingual title-page of William Hastie's album
of 1798 presented to Tsar Paul I.
National Library of Russia, St Petersburg.

Printed and bound in Italy by Grafiche Milani

CONTENTS

The author, Lyuba Semikina and Anna Galichenko on the terrace at Alupka, April 2001.

Dedicated to:

Terence Reeves-Smyth; Marcus Wheeler;
and to the memory of Lyubov Vasilyevna Semikina:
each of whom played a large part in this voyage of discovery.

INTRODUCTION

This book has its origins in a Black Sea holiday cruise from Constantinople to Salonika, by way of the Bosphorus, Trebizond, and Sebastopol, in September 2000. I had been mildly aware, before we set off, that Edward Blore had built a palace on the shores of the Crimea; I had armed myself with a copy of Professor Mordaunt Crook's article about it of 1972 in *Country Life*; otherwise, I was totally ignorant of the part played by English and Scottish architects and craftsmen in South Russia. I was entranced both by Alupka and Bakhchisaray, despite the fact that our visits, at the height of the holiday season, were cursory, incomplete, and overcrowded: and resolved to return for a better look.

Before doing so, I sought to read up on the subject. I was astonished to discover that no book has ever been published on Edward Blore and his works. Whilst he could be a very pedestrian architect at his worst, I still think that his best work is greatly under-rated. In the absence of any authoritative work, I derived much assistance from Hugh Meller's unpublished thesis of 1974 and from Terence Reeves-Smyth's unpublished essay of 1982 on Crom Castle and its demesne. Though first, Tamara Talbot-Rice; then Isobel Rae; then Professors Cross and Shvidkovsky; have written extensively and informatively about the British in North Russia, nobody, in either country or in either language, seems to have written about their work in South Russia. So I resolved to try to fill the gap: this book is the result.

I returned to Yalta in April 2001 – just before the start of the holiday season, but in time for the first of the spring flowers – accompanied by Terence Reeves-Smyth, garden historian and archaeologist. We spent a fruitful and enjoyable week in private holiday flats in the village of Alupka; despite the fact that neither of us spoke Russian, and nobody on the staff at Alupka spoke English, we contrived to learn a great deal – partly through our guide and interpreter, the late Lyubov Semikina; partly from the palace historian, Anna Galichenko, who speaks some French; and partly through our own powers of observation. We were greeted with the utmost kindness and courtesy, and shown everything we wished to see. At Bakhchisaray, we were shown around by its English-speaking then Assistant Director, Alexis Haiworonsky. At Alupka, we were allowed into the bedrooms; onto the leads of the roof; around the basements; and even, at my request, had the Okhrana seal struck from the door of the former kitchen, now used as a store-room. Moreover, we were taken to see many of the other houses and palaces of architectural significance in the Crimea.

My greatest regret is, that I came to this (to me, at any rate) fascinating field of study so late in life. I should have wished to learn Russian; and to travel to St Petersburg, Moscow, Odessa, and Simferopol, to examine for myself the drawings and documents there. But alas, age, and a degree of ill health, have rendered this impracticable. I am deeply grateful to Lyubov Semikina, who sent me the texts of many essential documents in Russian; and to Marcus Wheeler, lately Professor of Slavonic Studies at the Queen's University of Belfast, for so kindly translating them for me. It is because of this shortcoming on my part that I have been compelled to use direct quotation from translations of the works of other authors, both in and out of copyright, to a greater extent than is considered usual in works of this kind. I can but hope that both the quick and the dead will consider my quotations fair and, in the circumstances, reasonable: and will forgive me. My earnest hope is that this little book will cause some younger, Russian-speaking, researcher to explore its subject-matter in greater depth; or, perhaps, induce some Crimean scholar to pursue the subject.

The plan of this book has been, first, to set out the context, historical and geographical, within which it is placed; then to give brief sketches of the characters of the principal personalities who governed the history; then to describe the palace of Bakhchisaray, and those concerned with its building and restoration; next to describe the palace of Alupka, and the several personalities concerned in one way or another in its construction; and finally, to discuss some lesser buildings in the Crimea in which Englishmen or Scotsmen had a hand.

My thanks are due to a number of individuals and institutions. First and foremost, to Terence Reeves-Smyth, who accompanied me throughout our trip to the Crimea; to Lyubov Vasilyevna Semikina, who was our guide and interpreter, became our friend, and who, since we parted, provided much help and support by e-mail until her sad death of leukemia after a long-drawn-out illness, in February 2004. Then, to Marcus Wheeler, who has provided me with a most punctual and efficient translation service from the Russian; then, to Dianne Williams, who has remedied my many shortcomings as a computer performer.

Next, I must very warmly thank all those who made our stay in the Ukraine so fruitful and enjoyable: Nadya Postoyenko, of Odessa, who made all our travel and accommodation arrangements; K. K. Kasperovich, Director of the Alupka Museum and Park; Anna Galichenko and Galina Filatova, his research staff; Vladimir Dmitrenko, photographer; and Marina Lenkova, librarian at Alupka. Also Alexis Haiworonsky, until very lately Assistant

Director of the Bakhchisaray Museum of History and Local Lore, now with the Crimean Ministry of Culture in Simferopol.

Then, Professor Alexander Worontsoff-Dashkov and Mrs Carmen de Pinies in the United States of America; M. Jacques Ibry of Paris; Angus Fowler of Marburg, Germany; Ann-Martha Rowan of the Irish Architectural Archive, Dublin; and the Trustees of the Thomas Damman Junior Memorial Trust of Dublin, who gave much-appreciated financial support to our travels.

Nearer home, I must gratefully acknowledge the help of Sir Howard Colvin; Professor A. G. Cross; Professor and Mrs George Huxley; Professor and Mrs Peter Jupp; David Walker of Edinburgh; Andor Gomme; John Killen of the Linen Hall Library, Belfast; Karen Latimer of the Queen's University Libraries, Belfast; Charles Newton of the Victoria and Albert Museum Print-Room, and Dr John Physick, formerly of that institution; Mr Simon Sebag-Montefiore, for permission to quote extensively from his admirable book on Prince Potemkin; Lucy Porten of the RIBA Drawings Collection and Trevor Todd of the RIBA Library; Dr C. G. Thomas of the Slavonic and East European Collection, the British Library; and Gordon Wheeler, lately of the Queen's University Library, Belfast.

To all of these, I wish to express my sincere appreciation. None of them should be held responsible for any errors this book may contain, for which I accept full responsibility.

Finally, I am very grateful to the Open Russia Foundation; the Paul Mellon Centre for Studies in British Art; the Marc Fitch Fund; the Esmé Mitchell Trust; and the Scouloudi Foundation in association with the Institute of Historical Research; for the generous financial assistance which has made possible this publication; and also those institutions and individuals (particularly my friend Terence Reeves-Smyth, and Christopher Sykes) who have kindly accorded me permission to reproduce illustrations without fee or payment.

C. E. B. B.
April 2004

DRAMATIS PERSONAE

RULERS; PATRONS; GARDENERS, CRAFTSMEN, ARCHITECTS

in order of year of birth, where known

Elizabeth I	b 1709 s 1741 d 1762	William Gould	b c. 1735 d 1812
Peter III	b 1728 s 1762 d 1762	Thomas Harrison	b 1744 d 1829
Catherine II (the Great)	b 1729 s 1762 d 1796	Charles Cameron	b 1745 d 1812
Prince Potemkin	b 1739 d 1791	William Hastie	b c. 1755 d 1832
Count Simon Vorontsov	b 1744 d 1832	Francis Heiton	b ? d 1833
Paul I	b 1754 s 1796 d 1801	Philip Elson	b 1785 d 1867
Alexander I	b 1777 s 1801 d 1825	William J Hunt	b ? d ?
Prince Michael Vorontsov	b 1781 d 1856	Edward Blore	b 1787 d 1879
Nicholas I	b 1796 s 1825 d 1855		
Alexander II	b 1818 s 1855 d 1881	*Crimean War* 1853–1856	

FOREWORD

Mark Girouard

In the high days of the nineteenth century, when Britain was the workshop of the world, exporting across the oceans steam engines and the rails for them to run on, metal products from ironclads to urinals, Manchester cloth to 'Christianize the nakedness of the heathen', hydraulic lifts, gasworks, waterworks and tramway systems for cities from Odessa to Buenos Ayres, along with less material products such as organized games, sea-bathing, the cold bath, the gentleman's club and the British nanny, the exports included a small but heavyweight line in country houses – for the British country house, and the life lived in it, were universally admired and emulated.

When I was working on my book on Victorian houses, I included a very provisional list of these, and got intrigued by the idea of architects in their London offices dispatching sheaves of drawings to remote and sometimes exotic locations, which they seldom visited themselves, hoping that these would materialise into real buildings, as they sometimes did, but perhaps more often did not. Architects with foreign commissions had to make a fundamental decision: should they give their buildings a stylistic flavour suitable to their foreign location, or should they keep them resolutely British? On the whole, they seem to have taken the latter decision, presumably on the grounds that their clients had employed them because they admired British country houses, and that was what they were going to get. So Paxton and Stokes provided Baron James de Rothschild with designs for a resolutely neo-Elizabethan mansion at Ferrières in France – only to have the drawings returned to them, and be made to produce something much less Elizabethan, but only marginally more French. With more success, Edward Buckton Lamb, commissioned in the 1850s to design a schloss for Graf Harrach at Hrádek in the Czech Republic, took a copy of Nash's *Mansions in England in the Olden Time* and transposed the interiors illustrated in it, almost moulding for moulding – to the delight, it would seem, of his clients, who had perhaps asked for this in the first place.

The exotic Mozarabic dress given by J. T. Knowles to Palacio Monserrate at Sintra in Portugal around 1860, is an example of the other approach. So, even more, is the bravura with which Edward Blore reacted to the amazing mountain landscape and Muslim traditions of the southern Crimea at Alupka. Blore's work in England has never excited me; but the combination of an exotic commission, a discriminating patron, apparently unlimited funds, superb craftsmen and a site for architects to dream of, stimulated him to produce his masterpiece. It is too-little-known in England; and it is a delight to have its complex story disentangled and its quality illuminated by the knowledge and enthusiasm of Sir Charles Brett – with, amongst the side dishes to the main course, the oriental pavilions of the sixteenth-century palace of Bakhchisaray (where Catherine the Great and Potemkin stayed on their famous Crimean tour) and neo-oriental and neo-classical buildings by the gifted Anglo-Russian architect Philip Elson.

When I first met Charlie Brett, he was working, superbly impervious to the dangers and difficulties of his native city in the 1960s, on his study of the buildings of Belfast. One of the agreeable side products of writing this foreword is that it has sent me back to re-read that pioneering work. Forty years on, with a full and distinguished career behind him, the zest, knowledge and wit with which he illuminated Belfast moves effortlessly to the mountains of the Crimea and is as fresh and as enjoyable as ever.

Mark Girouard
June 2004

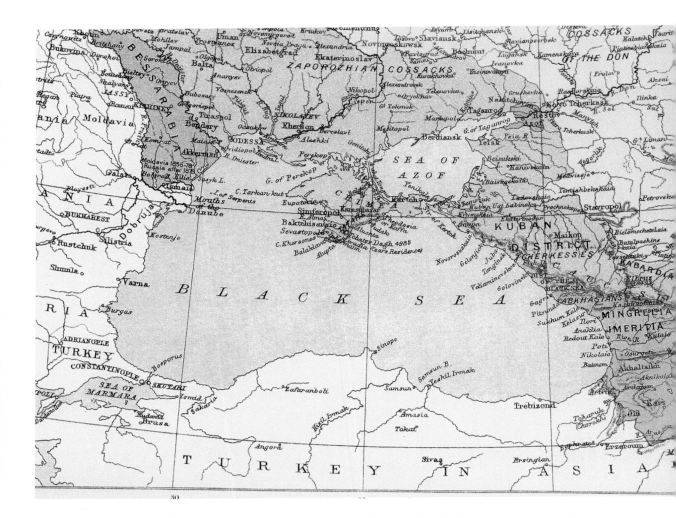

1. Map of Southern Russia 1682–1914: the area coloured yellow is the ancient territory of Russia; the small patch coloured brown, around Rostov, was acquired under the Empress Anne (1730–1740); the large area coloured red was acquired in the reign of Catherine the Great (1762–1795); the areas coloured purple-grey were acquired under the Tsar Alexander I (1801–1825); and the area coloured green was acquired thereafter.

From *An Historical Atlas of Modern Europe, 1789–1922*, by Sir Charles Grant Robertson (OUP, 1924), by permission of Oxford University Press.

I: PREAMBLE

A. RUSSIA AND THE WEST

Is, or was, Russia part of Europe? That is one of the greatest conundrums of the period. Certainly Peter the Great, Elizabeth, and Catherine thought that it was: indeed, Catherine expressly said so, in her famous 'Instructions' of 1767: "Russia is a European power".[1] But her successors, especially Nicholas I, "regarded 'Russia' and 'Europe' as two distinct entities. 'Europe' was evil; 'Russia' was virtuous: a distinction which he made clear in his manifesto announcing the execution of the Decembrists on 13th July 1826".[2] "We Russians have two fatherlands", wrote Dostoevsky, "Russia and Europe".

Attitudes towards the several countries of western Europe fluctuated according to circumstances. The empress Elizabeth much favoured the French; and their influence was predominant during her reign. Italian architects such as Quarenghi, Rastrelli and Rinaldi flourished; the Germans were less popular, except for gardeners; and the Swedes highly unpopular. The British were on the whole not much liked: except for Charles Cameron, a Scotsman who professed Jacobite connections (dishonestly, as it turns out). These contradictions lasted into the reign of Nicholas I: "with Britain, Nicholas' relations were perhaps the most confusing of all. He was something of an anglophile and loved the life of an English country gentleman. But he did not comprehend the political system within which British diplomats were obliged to work, and he found the institution of Parliament and its political debates incomprehensible".[3] As elsewhere in Europe, Lord Byron and Sir Walter Scott were widely read in Russia. But ever since the mid-eighteenth century France had been the predominant influence, a process accelerated by an influx of refugees from the French Revolution. As Martha Wilmot wrote to her father in 1806, "Never was a Land so over-run with Locusts as this with french ... Dancing Masters are of course french, so are multitudes of Physicians ... taylors, Mantua-makers, Milliners, Waiting Maids, Cooks, Booksellers &c. &c. &c. &c. swarm with french, & as for Education that of the youth of Russia has been *exclusively* in their hands".[4] In another letter of 1806, her sister Catherine wrote "The English

---

[1]   Lincoln, *Nicholas I*, 1978, p. 50.
[2]   *Ibid.*, p. 250.
[3]   *Ibid.*, p. 331.
[4]   Wilmot, *Russian Journals*, 1934, p. 275.

1

Nation abstractedly is respected, but its practices are unknown, its Language rarely spoken, its fashions disliked, & the individuals criticised in a manner absolutely different from any other ... I am as well convinced that thro' Novels, Hairdressers, Tutoresses, Abbés, Cooks, & Milliners Russia will be revolutionised by France before twenty years roll over their heads".[1] Tolstoy remarked that the qualities of the upper class required first-class French; long, well-kept and polished nails, and a constant expression of elegant and contemptuous *ennui*.

This preference for France and things French was further accentuated after the Treaty of Tilsit in 1807, when Alexander I joined Bonaparte in the Continental Blockade against Britain; but in 1810 Russia refused to close her ports to neutral ships. Not surprisingly, amicable relations with France were reversed by Napoleon's invasion of Russia and the burning of Moscow by Count Rostopchin, to deny the city to the enemy, in 1812, a great watershed in the culture of Russia's upper classes. Thereafter, for some years the French were disliked, though their language was still the language of polite society, and manners and dress styles still came from Paris. "Russian noblemen gave up Cliquot and Lafite for *kvas* and vodka, *haute cuisine* for cabbage soup".[2] The British, and perhaps especially the Scots, were more popular now: and Anglophiles were not as rare as they had previously been. The Grand Tour, in reverse, became a prerequisite for the sprigs of Russian nobility; "Russians flocked to the sceptred isle to educate themselves in the latest fashions and the designs of its fine houses, to acquire new techniques of estate management and landscape gardening, and to buy *objets d'art,* carriages and wigs".[3] The Gothic and Tudor settings of Sir Walter Scott's novels were widely admired, and the architecture of the period began to creep into fashion. As Professor Shvidkovsky has justly remarked, "The development of Russian neo-Gothic in the classical period came to a climax in one of the most splendid ensembles of southern Russia, Count Vorontsov's palace at Alupka on the Crimean coast, built in 1832 by Edward Blore".[4] But, much earlier than this, a considerable body of English craftsmen and professional people had arrived in Russia.

Soon after the formal annexation to Russia of the Crimea in the summer of 1783, Catherine the Great and Prince Potemkin had determined to build a new Black Sea fleet, for which an adequate base, and ship-building facilities, would be necessary. The youthful Nikolai Ivanovich Korsakov had been sent to England in 1775, and had spent two years there, industriously studying under the best engineers and manufacturers of the day, John Smeaton: Josiah Wedgwood; the

---

[1]   *Ibid.*, p. 216.
[2]   Figes, *Natasha's Dance*, 2002, p. 67.
[3]   *Ibid.*, p. 62.
[4]   Shvidkovsky, *The Empress and the Architect*, 1996, p. 223.

owners of the Carron Ironworks; and iron-master John Wilkinson. "Korsakov's skills were soon employed in surveying the site of the new port and shipyard on the Black Sea itself. As a result of his findings, it was decided to transform the little Tatar village of Akhtiyar into Sevastopol".[1]

The Russian Navy, for which inland peasants were manifestly unsuited, was for the most part manned by Greek sailors, and officered by the British. By 1855, five Englishmen (or Scotsmen) had risen to be Russian Admirals – Crown, Hamilton, Elphinstone, Dugdale, and Greig; and at least two other Russian Admirals had seen service in the Royal Navy – indeed, Admiral Lazaref had fought as a midshipman at Trafalgar. It was the Scotsman Thomas Mackenzie, who famously commanded one of the four fireships that gained the victory over the Turkish fleet at Chesmé, who was actually in command of the construction of the first harbour at Sevastopol, and who died there in 1786. "Mordvinov [an admiral married to an English girl] and Korsakov both are much more like Englishmen than any foreigners I ever met", wrote Lady Craven.[2]

The harbour itself was mainly the creation of a rather unsavoury character named John Upton, originally a building contractor and canal engineer from Gloucester, who got into trouble in 1819 for selling himself building materials; and in 1826 for "the grossest fraud and deception" on a Turnpike Trust; when prosecuted, he absconded, skipping bail; in 1828, he was working as contractor at Goodrich Court, Hereford, under Edward Blore, when he was forced by his creditors to flee the country. Perhaps Blore took a charitable view and offered him introductions in Russia: for he next turns up as a Lieutenant-Colonel of Engineers in the Russian Army, responsible for the actual construction of the docks at Sevastopol. Work started on 17th June 1832, and was not completed until 1853, though Upton had at the outset given an estimate of five years and two-and-a-half million roubles, a sum by far exceeded in the event. As the visiting Mr H. D. Seymour, later MP, was to write in 1855, "Those who have visited these works will not be astonished at the delay in completing them. Basins of a great size cut in the living rock, and cased with English cement, with gigantic locks, and such a length of aqueducts, tunnels, and other labours, both principal and accessory, are a justification of the engineer, who received the full approbation of the Emperor". And added, in a footnote: "It is but justice to Col. Upton, who is now no more, to observe, notwithstanding the reports lately circulated about certain faults in the early part of his life, that he enjoyed a good reputation among his own countrymen in Russia, and was considered a honest and faithful servant of his employer, while he has left monuments of his talents of which we may be proud".[3]

[1] Cross, *By the Banks of the Thames*, 1980, p. 184.
[2] Craven, *Journey through the Crimea to Constantinople*, 1814, p. 158.
[3] Seymour, *Russia on the Black Sea and Sea of Azov*, 1855, p. 69.

I: PREAMBLE

Upton was, with his sons, reponsible for a number of significant harbour buildings, including the officers' library and reading rooms; the Maritime Assembly Rooms; the port's water supply system; the plan for the layout of the city centre; the so-called Count's Harbour, where Rear-Admiral Count M. I. Voynovich used to come ashore; and, in 1846, "a beautiful colonnade with two pavilions in antique style and a wide stone staircase. The niches in the pavilions were decorated with marble copies of antique statues, the lower part of the staircase was decorated with a pair of lions, made by the Italian sculptor F. Peliccio" (information from Mrs Semikina). One of his sons married a Russian lady, and was captured by the British and French at Balaklava, but permitted to remain on there. The father appears to have returned to England just before the outbreak of war, and died in London in 1853. The port came to prominence in the Crimean War, is still the principal Black Sea base both of the Russian and the Ukrainian fleets, although no longer a closed port, and is now regularly visited by Western cruise liners.

One of the first English gardeners to go to the Crimea, who was to become world-famous (J. C. Loudon acclaimed him as the Capability Brown of Russia: he was, in fact, Lancelot Brown's protégé) – was the Lancastrian, William Gould. He arrived in Russia in 1776, recruited by no less a personage than Catherine's favourite, the flamboyant but energetic Prince Grigory Potemkin. He was only one, if the most distinguished, of a sizeable group of English gardeners who came to Russia: John Bush and his son Joseph, employed from 1779 at Tsarskoe Selo, hospitable and popular, whose daughter married Charles Cameron; James Meader, from Alnwick, who came to Peterhof in the same year; James Hackett and James Sparrow, both of whom worked at Gatchina from 1779 onwards; Francis Reid and John Munro, who worked at Tsaritsyno.[1] All these people described themselves as 'gardeners'. Nowadays, most of them would probably describe themselves as 'landscape architects'. They were eventually somewhat superseded by German gardeners: but there is no doubt that from the beginning to the end of Catherine's reign the English style of gardening was the predominant fashion. In 1772, the Empress herself wrote to Voltaire: "J'aime à la folie présentement les jardins à l'anglaise, les lignes courbes, les pentes douces, les étangs en forme de lacs, les archipels en terre fermé, et j'ai un profond mépris pour les lignes droites, les allées jumelles ... en un mot, l'anglomanie domine ma plantomanie".[2] Loudon says, in 1834, "The garden-artists of Russia are the English or German head-gardeners attached to the establishment of the emperor, or of some eminent noble. Gould, Potemkin's gardener, was the Brown of Russia in Catherine's time. This man

[1]   Shvidkovsky, 1996, *op. cit.*, pp. 4, 5.
[2]   Cross, *op. cit.*, p. 266; and Voltaire *Correspondence*, ed. Besterman, LXXXII, 1963, p. 130.

had a character in some degree analagous to that of his master; he lived in splendour, kept horses and carriages, and gave occasionally entertainments to the nobility. He afterwards returned to England, and died, at an advanced age, in 1816, at Ormskirk in Lancashire, his native town". But adds: "A foreigner once established as head-gardener to the emperor, or any of the first nobility in Russia, becomes in some degree a despot, like his master; and, unless he commits very gross errors indeed, his conduct is never enquired into, nor does he lose his place but with life, unless he wishes to return home. He is not very liberally paid, but he enjoys every comfort the state of society there affords; lives in a house that would be reckoned a considerable mansion in England, and has abundance of servants, and a carriage and horses, at his command. His country, and his broad cloth, procure him the respect of the nobles, and the dread of the slaves: the former he may render tributary by presents of seeds, and the latter he may kick and beat at pleasure. If at any time he goes too far, a few radishes to the police-bailiffs, or a few peaches, or a melon, to the chevaliers their masters, will restore everything to harmony".[1]

Prince Potemkin was unconventional in his conduct towards his gardeners: "It was a mark of his Anglomania that Potemkin clearly regarded an English gardener as the equal of a Russian aristocrat: such was his respect for these lords of the flowerbed that he dined at the Bushes' with two of his nieces, one of their husbands Count Skavronsky, and three ambassadors, a social puzzle that alarmed a supposedly more democratic English visitor".[2] (It should be remembered, however, that Mrs Bush had a reputation as an exceptionally good cook; and the Prince liked his victuals.)

Gould's principal task was to lay out the grounds of Potemkin's Taurida Palace on the outskirts of St Petersburg, built to designs by Starov between 1782 and 1790. According to Loudon, "the natural surface of the ground was flat, and in many parts, a bog ... The garden was planned and superintended by William Gould, from Lancashire, who displayed great judgment in forming the ponds, out of which he got sufficient material to make an agreeable variety of swells and declivities." Gould was "a prominent and colourful figure in the British community in St Petersburg, a character with a fund of frequently scurrilous anecdotes, a man whose 'true English honesty, excellent heart, and hospitality, claim the esteem of all ranks'".[3] But "There was something of Haroun-al-Rashid about Potemkin ... Gould's extraordinary speciality was building English gardens overnight, on the spot, wherever Potemkin stayed. Most historians have presumed that the stories of Potemkin's instant gardens were simply legends – it

---

[1] Loudon, *Encyclopaedia of Gardening*, 1834, p. 265.
[2] *Ibid.*, p. 249.
[3] Cross, *By the Banks of the Neva*, 1997, p. 276; and Porter, *Travelling Sketches*, 1809, I, p. 58.

was surely impossible that Gould travelled with a convoy of oak trees, rockeries and shrubberies. But here Legend and Reality merge: the State Archives in Petersburg, which contain Potemkin's accounts, show that Gould constantly travelled with Potemkin to places where we know from other sources that these gardens were indeed laid out in a matter of days".[1]

And "Since the Prince could not live without his English gardens, the travels of his English gardener William Gould were a weathervane of Potemkin's intentions. In late 1786, the English 'Emperor of Gardens' set off for the south in style with his 'general staff' of gardeners and workmen. The cognoscenti knew this meant that something important was afoot. The Empress was about to depart on her grandiose journey to the Crimea to meet the Holy Roman Emperor under the gaze of Europe".[2] But, "during the reign of Paul" (after the death of Potemkin in 1791, and of Catherine the Great in 1796) Gould, who was deeply offended by the Emperor Paul's "unabated hatred for Potemkin that led him to turn the [Taurida] palace into a stables for the horseguards and to neglect the gardens, retired to England",[3] where he died at Ormskirk, a wealthy man, in 1816.

B. THE CRIMEA

Taurida, known in England as Crim Tartary, now known as the Crimea, was in antiquity occupied by Scythians - whose very beautiful jewellery and metalwork is preserved in the excellent archaeological museum in Odessa. (They are to be called Scythians, with a hard 'c', as the admirable young curatrix told me; not with a soft 'c' as in scythe; but as in 'scandal'). It is an almost-island, hanging below the steppes of Russia: much as the Isle of Wight hangs down beneath England: but very much larger in extent, covering nearly 10,000 square miles compared to 150 square miles. Its northern slopes are a continuation of the Ukrainian steppe: rising gradually, through limestone hills dotted with Scythian burial-mounds, to a range of mountains over 5,000 feet high (subject to snow, hailstorms and frost in winter; to parched dust in summer): the latter sharply divide the northern Crimea from the Russian Riviera to the south of the mountains, which enjoys a Mediterranean climate, where cypresses, olives, vines, figs, magnolias, tulip trees, and fruit trees flourish, and only light, and soon melting, snowfalls occur each winter.

By degrees, the peninsula's coastal regions were colonised by the Greeks, who found its climate not too dissimilar from their homeland. Here they established trading posts, and grew crops of wheat, fruit, and wine. Taurida loomed large in Greek mythology, for here according to Euripides, Iphigeneia

---

[1]   Montefiore, *Prince of Princes*, 2000, p. 306.
[2]   *Ibid.*, p. 347.
[3]   Cross, *By the Banks of the Thames*, 1980, p. 176.

was banished by the Gods, and here her brother Orestes landed. For the Romans, too, the Euxine (or Black Sea) was an important souce of corn; not far away, on the shores of what is now Bulgaria, Ovid served out his wearisome exile. Later still, the Genoese established trading outposts around its coastline. In 1779, Gluck's most successful opera, *Iphigénie en Tauride*, was performed in Paris for the first time. The Black Sea still has its literary resonances: as W. B. Yeats in 1930 described it in his poem 'Byzantium', "that dolphin-torn, that gong-tormented sea": and indeed, whatever about the gongs, dolphins can still be seen playing in the sea far below the high terraces of the palace at Alupka.

After the decline and collapse of the Roman Empire, first came the Goths in AD 250, the Huns (376), the Khazars (eighth century), the Byzantine Greeks (1016), the Polovtsians or Kipchaks (1050), and finally the Mongols in 1237. These last were the Tatars, survivors of the Golden Horde, who established an independent Khanate under the Geray dynasty which descended directly from Genghis Khan. Their empire flourished from the fifteenth to the seventeenth century, but after falling into the Ottoman sphere of influence, it subsequently suffered much from the wars between Turkey and Russia. The Tatars made looting raids northwards, as far as Kiev and Moscow; the Russians made retaliatory raids southwards into Ottoman territory; but, for the most part, the Cossacks of the steppes, a warlike people disinclined to agriculture which they regarded as a female occupation, acted as a barrier between the two. Finally, in 1777, the Russian general Suvorov defeated the Ottoman armies, and in 1783 Prince Potemkin accepted the surrender of the last of the Khans of Crim Tartary, and the Crimea was incorporated into New Russia. Astoundingly, he succeeded in pacifying the Cossacks, attracting their personal loyalty, and resettling most of them elsewhere, so setting free for new settlements the rich dark soil they had been fruitlessly occupying. There followed an influx of foreigners – mostly Russian, but also Germans, Jews, Mennonites from Danzig, and Greeks, attracted by the liberal policies of Potemkin and Catherine the Great, gifts of land, money and livestock, and promises of religious freedom of conscience.

The remaining Tatars, all Sunni Muslims, increasingly came to resent the presence of these strangers, by whom, before long, they were outnumbered. There was a growing hostility between the races. Tsar Nicholas I could write: "There is nothing poorer and more lazy than these southern Tatars. If the Crimea was not in Tatar hands, then everything would be entirely different, for where there are Russian or Little Russian serf-owners and settlers ... there is grain". Not everybody shared that view of the indigenous Tatars, however: the Crimean War of 1853 and "the laws of 1860–63 and 1874 caused an exodus of the Crimean Tatars; they abandoned their admirably irrigated fields and gardens, and moved to Turkey, so that now [1911] their number falls below

2. *Interior of a Tartar School at Alupka*, gouache by Carlo Bossoli, of 1843. Count Vorontsov's palace, and the mosque he built the local Tatar inhabitants, are both visible behind the pupils in the wide opening onto the veranda. The building appears typica Tatar styles of architecture at the period.

Bossoli had been born in Lugano in 1815; but in 1820 his father, an engineer, had moved with his family to Odessa. As a boy was taken up by Countess Vorontsov, studied in Rome, and on his return, in his twenties, was commissioned by her to paint vi of Alupka and the Crimea. He returned to Italy in 1843, and became a highly successful painter, patronised by (amongst oth Queen Victoria.

Reproduced from the original in a private collection by permission of Sayn-Wittgenstein Fine Art Inc., of New York.

100,000 ... Those of the south coast, mixed with Greeks and Italians, are well known for their skill in gardening, their honesty, and their laborious habits, as well for their fine features, presenting the Tatar type at its best".[1]

By reason principally of the difference in climate, the architecture of the Crimea is quite out of the mainstream of Russian architecture. Throughout northern Russia, the paramount consideration is shelter and protection from the bitter winters. In the southern Ukraine, and especially on the riviera south of the coastal range of mountains in the Crimea, it is coolness and shade, protection from the summer heats. Tatar building traditions were largely

---

[1]   *Encyclopaedia Britannica*, 11th edn, 1911, XXVI, p. 448.

3. Vernacular Tatar architecture in the Crimea: native cottage at Alupka, engraved by (or after) Carlo Bossoli, 1854. Reproduced from the coloured print in the Alupka Archive; photograph by Vladimir Dmitrenko.

Ottoman or Persian in character: apart from the rare palace, fortress, or (less rare) mosque, the domestic buildings were for the most part of timber, with oversailing eaves or verandahs, wide openings, and little in the way of solid walls.

After the Tatar submission to Russia in 1783, a rather unsophisticated neo-classicism was the norm in the new cities such as Odessa. A smattering of it has survived the successive wars that have ravaged all the Black Sea littoral. A certain Byzantine influence is sometimes dimly discernible. There is little of the splendidly ornate classicism of Rastrelli, Quarenghi, or Charles Cameron in the eighteenth-century St Petersburg of the Empresses Elizabeth and Catherine; little of the onion domes and eccentricities of Moscow; little of the baroque; not very much of the Gothic, or Gothic Revival, styles, so alien to these southern shores. Even in Northern Russia, Gothic was a rarity: one of the few examples of the Revival was the palace created at Marfino, outside Moscow, by the architect Bykovsky for the Countess Sofia Panin between 1830 and her death in

9

1846. But it does not seem to have had much influence, direct or indirect, on Crimean architecture.

Accordingly, Bakhchisaray and Alupka, the two major buildings with which this little book is principally concerned, are each altogether *sui generis*; and, not only is each far outside the mainstream of Russian architecture, each is outside the mainstream even of Crimean architecture. As Shiryaev, in his *Crimean Estate Architecture* put it, "The architecture of the Alupka palace, which appears to us an idiosyncratic symbiosis of neo-Gothic and Orientalising elements, connected moreover with the duality of the artistic conception of feudal castle and baroque villa, stands absolutely apart in Russian architecture of the 1830s – 1840s". And indeed, it stands apart as an extraordinarily unusual building in European terms.

After the Revolution of 1917, and the ensuing famines, the remaining Tatars still constituted a quarter of the population of the Crimea in 1923; but continuing friction between the Tatar and the Russian elements of the population led some of the Tatars to side with the German invaders in 1943, and by order of Stalin some 238,000 were deported to Central Asia in the following year. They were officially cleared of the accusation of treason in 1967, but only a fairly small number have succeeded in returning to the Crimea.

The Crimea had become part of the Ukraine in 1953, when Nikita Kruschev wished to celebrate the three hundredth anniversary of the union of the Ukraine with Russia rather than with Poland. In 1991, the Ukraine voted to declare itself independent from Russia, against the wishes of most of the population of the Crimea; the Crimean Parliament voted to become an autonomous republic; then in 1992 it voted for complete independence; which was not however accorded by Kiev. So the Crimea, at the time of writing, remains a semi-autonomous state within the Republic of Ukraine.[1]

---

[1] Bennigsen and Wimbush, *Muslims of the Soviet Empire*, 1985, p. 240.

4. The 'Asiatic Pavilion', Alupka. This quite modest house was used by the Vorontsov family, and their guests, whilst the palace at Alupka was a-building. The design is attributed by some authorities to Philip Elson, but it is very much in the local Tatar tradition, with wide eaves and verandas. It is still standing, though so altered and mutilated as to be unrecognisable. Behind it appears the mosque, also attributed to Elson (now demolished), built by Count Vorontsov as part of the bargain when he acquired from the villagers the land for his palace.

From a lithograph of 1830 by Wolff in the Alupka Archive, photograph by Vladimir Dmitrenko.

5. Another view of the Asiatic Pavilion, also from a contemporary engraving by Wolff, from the Alupka Archive, photograph by Vladimir Dmitrenko.

C. THE EMPOWERORS

It has seemed sensible, since most of this work is concerned with the lives and doings of the relatively unimportant, to give some account of the three enormously wealthy, and indeed all-powerful, individuals who made possible the by no means inconsiderable achievements of the professional men and skilled artisans who worked for them. By far the most important, during the period in question, were: the Empress Catherine the Great; the 'Prince of Princes', Grigory Potemkin; and the Count, later Prince, Michael Vorontsov. What follows, by way of introduction, is an attempt to provide a cursory thumb-nail sketch of the life and career of each of the three, for the benefit of those readers who may not already know more about them than I do. I have thought it better not to foot-note this brief chapter; my notes on Catherine the Great are drawn principally from the writings of Isabel de Madariaga, those on Prince Potemkin on those of Montefiore, and of Ligne's biographer Mansel, those on Vorontsov on the writings of Rhinelander.

1. CATHERINE II OF ALL THE RUSSIAS ('THE GREAT'): 1729–1796

The Empress Catherine, by birth the Princess Sophia of Zerbst-Anhalt, was born in Stettin, into a minor German princely house, in 1729. In 1745, when she was sixteen, she was married to the Grand Duke Peter Fyodorovich of Russia, nominated heir to the throne and a grandson, if a rather ineffectual one, of Peter the Great. Although the marriage was probably unconsummated, a son, the future Tsar Paul I, was born in 1754; it has never been certain who was his father. Peter III succeeded his great-aunt, the Empress Elizabeth, on her death in 1762. But he was not to rule for long: drunken, brutal and ineffectual, he was strangled in June 1762, with the connivance of Catherine. "It made Catherine notorious in Europe as an adulterous regicide ... Catherine ... issued a much-mocked statement blaming Peter's death on 'a haemorrhoidal colic'. This absurd if necessary diagnosis was to become a euphemism in Europe for political murder" (Montefiore).

Catherine had begun learning Russian at the age of fourteen, on her betrothal; and, though brought up a Lutheran, had herself instructed in the rites of the Russian Orthodox Church. When she converted to Orthodoxy, she changed her name, at the wish of the Empress Elizabeth, to Catherine – Ekaterina – because the name Sophia called up unhappy memories of Peter the Great's half-sister who had conspired against him. "It was her determination to become a Russian in order that she might the better rule in Russia, and she succeeded. She acquired a full command of all the resources of the language, and a no less complete understanding of the nature of the Russian people". In politics, she was, at any rate at first, more enlightened and liberal than many of her predecessors or successors; though her liberalism waned somewhat after the

6. The young and glamorous Empress Catherine, aged 33, on the night of 28 June 1762, wearing a green uniform of the Preobrazhensky Guards hastily borrowed from a Captain Talyzin, and mounted on her thoroughbred grey stallion 'Brilliant', sets out on the March to Peterhof in order to seize power from her husband the Tsar Peter III. A somewhat idealised, and retrospective, portrait, which nevertheless conveys vividly the charisma which was to enlist the loyalty of the twelve-thousand imperial guards who rallied immediately to her revolution – including the guardsman Grigory Potemkin.
Musée des Beaux-Arts, Chartres, France, by permission of the Bridgeman Art Library.

French Revolution. Having been educated by French governesses, she corresponded, amongst others, with Voltaire, and declared her adherence to the Age of Reason. She admired English democracy, architecture, landscaping, and the arts. Though professing the beliefs of the Russian Orthodox Church, in fact she adhered to the tenets of no religious belief, and accorded an uncommon degree of religious liberty to her subjects, even (unusually amongst Western rulers) Jews and Muslims: she made a point of paying courtesy calls on the Mullahs in every Mohammedan town she visited. Of morals, she had no more than an alley-cat; she was very highly sexed, a most lascivious lady, who nonetheless never allowed her lusts to master her intellect. Many of her closest advisers became her lovers; many of her lovers became her advisers. With her closest adviser of all, Potemkin, she remained in love even after he had ceased to be her lover .

She was an exceptionally splendid monarch, popular within Russia, and feared elsewhere. Enormously rich, she was able to indulge every desire. She deserves to stand amongst the great queens of history – Queen Elizabeth I of England; the Archduchess Maria Theresa; Queen Victoria. She died of a stroke, aged sixty-seven, on 10 November 1796, and was succeeded by her son Paul, who sought forthwith to reverse everything she had stood for, and who was assassinated in 1801. He in turn was succeeded by his sons, Alexander I who reigned until 1825, and thereafter Nicholas I, who was to continue on the throne until 1855. Neither was to exhibit the talents of his grandmother.

2. PRINCE GRIGORY ALEXANDROVICH POTEMKIN (1739–1791)

Grigory Potemkin was born near Smolensk, third child in a family of the minor gentry, of Polish descent, which owned a modest acreage and 430 male serfs. His father, according to Montefiore, was "an oafish military eccentric ... This early Russian prototype of Colonel Blimp was almost insane, permanently indignant and recklessly impulsive". The boy was educated at Moscow University, where at first he flourished; but was expelled for idleness, and non-attendance at lectures, in 1760, when he borrowed the fare from a friend and joined the Horse-Guards Regiment at St Petersburg. Whilst on guard duty, a chance meeting with the future Empress Catherine led to promotion, and she continued to take an interest in the career of this tall and handsome young guardsman, in 1762 appointing him a Gentleman of the Bedchamber. In the following year, he had the misfortune of losing the sight in his right eye, and in consequence, stayed away from court for eighteen months.

In the first Russo-Turkish war of 1769, he became a major-general of cavalry at the age of 29, and returned to St Petersburg a war hero: during his short stay, he is said to have dined with the Empress eleven times. Three years later, he earned the "undying hostility" of Count Simon Vorontsov, who

7. Prince Potemkin, painted in St Petersburg in about 1790 by Johann Baptist von Lampi, not long before his death aged 52 on 5th October 1791.

Hermitage Museum, St Petersburg, by permission of the Bridgeman Art Library.

suffered the indignity of having his Grenadiers rescued by Potemkin from 12,000 Turkish cavalry; soon after, the tables were turned; but each resented the obligation to the other. It seems that it was only after the end of that war that he became Catherine's lover *en titre*, in 1774.

The Prince de Ligne, who had known all the great men of his day, from Frederick the Great to Napoleon by way of Rousseau, Voltaire, and Marie Antoinette, described Potemkin as "The most extraordinary man I ever met ... what is the secret of his magic? Genius, genius and still more genius". He also painted an arresting portrait of this unusual man: Ligne's biographer quotes: "the most extraordinary man there has ever been. A collection of contradictions, he made diagrams with diamonds, had no desk but his knees, no comb but his fingers ... With one hand making signals to women who attracted him, with the other signs of the Cross ... He wore either a dirty dressing-gown or a superb tunic covered in orders and diamonds as big as fists ... fantastic in his hours, his meals, his sleep, and his tastes, wanting to have everything like a child and capable of doing without like a great man".[1]

Montefiore sums up his remarkable qualities as "primitive energy, an almost animalistic sexuality, outrageous originality, driving intellect and surprising sensitivity". Soon after becoming Catherine's lover, he was assigned rooms close to hers in the Winter Palace; promoted to be Lieutenant-Colonel of the Preobrazhensky Guards; and appointed Governor-General of New Russia. In 1776, he became a Prince of the Holy Roman Empire.

During the ensuing decade, the sexual relationship with Catherine waned; not so their mutual affection, though each proceeded to take new lovers, in his case including several of his nieces. He was enormously wealthy, thanks mostly to Catherine's generosity, but he made free also with the resources of the state as if they had been his own. Potemkin became preoccupied with the task of procuring for the Russian empire both the Crimea and the Caucasus, in which he was successful, and he was promoted to Field Marshal in 1784. The latter years of that decade were to prove the apogee of his career, culminating in the famous visitation to the Crimea of 1787.

In the autumn of 1791, Potemkin, in South Russia, became ill. In October, while travelling across the remote Bessarabian steppe, he had to be carried out of his coach and laid on the ground where, worn out and in great pain, he died, aged fifty-two. One of his Cossack escort is said to have remarked, pithily, "Lived on gold; died on grass". Catherine was inconsolable.

---

[1]   Montefiore, *Prince of Princes*, 2000, p. 8.

C. THE EMPOWERORS: COUNT VORONTSOV

3. COUNT (LATER PRINCE) MIKHAIL SEMYONOVICH VORONTSOV (1781–1856)

Michael Vorontsov, born at St Petersburg in 1781, was the son of Count Simon Vorontsov, Potemkin's rescuer and antagonist in 1772. As Montefiore (perhaps rather unkindly) put it of Count Simon, "This pudding-faced Anglophile was rightly regarded by Potemkin and Catherine as unreliable, and spent most of his career in honourable exile as Ambassador to London". Whether or no he was pudding-faced I cannot say; but he certainly, from his appointment in 1785, rendered considerable service to Russia during his many years in England, though he never learned English, and conversed (as was the fashion) in diplomatic French. Simon's sister was a distinguished scientist and scholar, Catherine Dashkova, who was exiled by Paul I on his accession because of her friendship with Catherine the Great. Although Simon Vorontsov was at first showered with honours by Paul I, he too was subsequently faced with dismissal and the forfeiture of all his property in Russia. This fate he prudently avoided by means of voluntary resignation and a plea of ill-health, and his estates were restored, and he was reappointed ambassador, by Paul's successor, in 1801. He was to remain in England for the rest of his life, dying only in 1832, having spent his later years living with his daughter Catherine, who had married the elderly Earl of Pembroke, at Wilton House.

Michael Vorontsov was educated privately (and very well) at the embassy, at 36 Harley Street in London; learning not only English, French and Russian, but also the classics, Hebrew – and joinery: for his father feared the spread of the French Revolution to Russia, and thought his son should have a trade. On attaining his majority, he set off for Russia "with a single suitcase and without servants" (Mikeshin). He was appointed a lieutenant in the élite Preobrazhensky Guards, and after a year in the capital, secured a transfer to the front; from 1805 he fought in Pomerania, and became a colonel; by 1810, after service against the Turks on the Danube, he had attained the rank of major-general. In 1812, he received a musket-ball wound in the thigh at the desperate fighting against Napoleon, in the defence of Moscow, at Borodino. Finally, he took part in the campaign of 1815, and in August of that year was appointed Commander in Chief of the Russian component of Wellington's allied army of occupation in northern France.

8 and 9 (facing pages overleaf). Count Mikhail Vorontsov, first painted as a young, dashing army officer, already appointed a major-general at the age of thirty-one. This portrait was painted in St Petersburg in 1812 by A. Molinari: presumably not long before the hard-fought battle of Borodino, in defence of Moscow against Napoleon, in which Vorontsov was quite seriously wounded in the thigh by a musket-ball (from the painting in the Alupka Archive). Secondly, painted by Sir Thomas Lawrence, on his visit to England to visit his father and sister soon after his marriage in Paris to Elizaveta Branitskaya in 1819. From 1815 until 1818 he had been General in command of the Russian army of occupation in France. He is painted in the uniform of a general, wearing the stars of the orders of St Alexander Nevsky, St Vladimir and St George.

Hermitage Museum, St Petersburg, by permission of the Bridgeman Art Library.

Somewhat surprisingly, in 1819 he chose to marry Elizaveta Branitskaya, the pretty and skittish great-niece of Prince Potemkin, despite the long-standing antagonism between the two families. She brought with her a substantial fortune to add to that which he had inherited from his wealthy uncle Alexander: and for the rest of his life, Michael Vorontsov was one of the richest men in Europe, with over 80,000 serfs on his several estates. Not that Vorontsov believed in serfdom: in 1820 he was involved in a scheme to free the serfs, starting with his own; but the Tsar would not hear of it. It comes as a surprise to learn, of such an aristocratic and military figure, that in the 1820s he was involved in (successful) negotiations, with business partners, to establish a stage-coach company contracted with the Post Office to provide services between Moscow and St Petersburg, and other towns. It comes, perhaps, as slightly less of a surprise to learn that in 1823 he built, on his estates, the first steam-ship to navigate the river Dnieper, with a thirty-horse-power engine; he and his wife "derived enormous enjoyment" from the astonishment of the riverains who could not understand how his vessel could steam upstream without sails or tow-rope. He was later to establish the first steam-ship service between the Black Sea ports. He was also fascinated by railways: it was to be a great disappointment in later years that he was never able to "overcome the inertia of the régime" and secure the construction of a proper railway network throughout Russia. He was, for a Russian aristocrat, unusually interested in promoting prosperity and the economy. Pushkin, who had his reasons for bearing malice, called him "half-milord, half-merchant", a description which Vorontsov would probably not have disowned.

In 1823, he was appointed Governor-General of the whole of New Russia (including the southern Ukraine and the Crimea) and Bessarabia: a position which he took exceedingly seriously, and which he was to hold for the unheard of period of thirty-one years. He chose Odessa for his official residence, and the Crimea for his home.

Whilst there, the Countess Elizaveta seems to have had a fling with the young poet Pushkin. As Binyon judiciously puts it, in a footnote, "The relationship between Pushkin and Elizaveta Vorontsova has been the subject of much dispute among scholars. Views range from that of T. G. Tsyavlovskaya ... who believes it to have been the most important and long-lasting affair of Pushkin's life ... and puts forward the hypothesis that Pushkin was the father of the Vorontsov's second daughter, Sofya ... to that of G. P. Makogonenko ... who denies that anything more than a mere acquaintance existed. Both positions seem extreme". It seems certain, however, that the Countess did take lovers; and, for that matter, that the Count had his mistresses, despite the almost Victorian austerity of his morals.

C. THE EMPOWERORS: COUNT VORONTSOV

His character has been quite controversial. His enemies, of whom he had not a few, regarded him as cold; austere; puritanical; and arrogant. His admirers, of whom also he had not a few, regarded him as honest; incorruptible; efficient; liberal; and public-spirited. Historians are divided: those who most admire Potemkin and Pushkin tend to the former view; those belonging to the English Whig tradition, including his nephew, Sydney Herbert, tend to the latter view as, on the whole, I do myself. The reasonably impartial H. D. Seymour, MP, writing during the Crimean War and shortly before the death of Prince Vorontsov, says "He displayed administrative qualities of the highest order, and possessed the rare quality of securing the affection and raising the tone of all around him. The soldiers admired him for his calm intrepidity, and loved him for his never-failing generosity and kindness, and the officers feared him for his inflexible justice ... I never yet have met an individual in whom the fundamental virtues of courage, prudence, generosity, and magnanimity were enhanced by such acute sagacity, such delicate refinement of sentiment, such simplicity of manners, and a modesty which when it survives the trial of power is the surest sign of a superior mind".

In later years, he was certainly a maddeningly methodical man. He got up every day at 7 am; worked till breakfast (of two boiled eggs and a slice of toast) at 8.30; from 9 until 3 he worked; then he went riding for daily exercise. By 6, he was impatiently awaiting dinner – usually roast beef and potatoes – with which he drank only water, though his guests were offered fine wines; but, after dinner, he drank one glass of "a very special, very old, sherry which he had inherited from his grandfather", and, with his coffee, smoked one Spanish cigarillo; then cards; one cup of tea at 11; and to bed on the dot of midnight. He drove his household hard. "His secretary Dondukov-Korsakov [who had to be ready to take dictation in English, French, or Russian] ... Baron Nicolay and various other aides, his son Simon, his wife Lise, his mistress Irma, his valet Giovanni, his groom Jim, his cook André, all ... admired and respected him deeply". But it can be understood why those of a more Bohemian character found him exasperating.

As to his building ventures, see below. He certainly seems to have been an uncommonly successful, and committed, administrator of South Russia. Between 1830 and 1832 Vorontsov had to cope with severe outbreaks of bubonic plague in Odessa, Bessarabia, and Sevastopol. Between 1820 and 1831, his son Alexander, his infant daughter, and his father all died. In 1844, he was promoted from Count to Prince; then Field Marshall; and General-Governor of the Caucasus. Thereafter, despite his age and increasing blindness, he was able to spend little time at his beloved palace and park of Alupka, being too busy conducting the (ultimately successful) wars against the local tribes in Daghestan and the Caucasus, and having to reside for the most part at Tiflis.

I: PREAMBLE

In 1853, the Crimean War broke out; and the Anglophile Vorontsov, acutely embarrassed by his conflict of loyalties in general, and in particular the fact that his nephew Sydney Herbert was the English Minister for War, tendered his resignation from all his public offices on grounds of ill-health, and retired to Odessa. Indeed, Herbert too was to suffer serious embarrassment because of his relationship with Vorontsov, his loyalty being questioned in Parliament: but without lasting ill-effects for his career. The Peace of Paris was signed on 30 March, 1856; but on 6 November of that year, Mikhail Vorontsov died, broken-hearted, at the age of seventy-four.

D: THE MARVELLOUS JOURNEY TO THE BLACK SEA

Few English gardeners, apart from William Gould, travelled far from St Petersburg. In June 1780, James Meader wrote that "Gould is gone to Astracan & the Ukraine to inspect into the Estate of Prince Potemkin his master, he promised me to collect every thing curious in the plant & animal way".[1] It was a few years later, however, after the annexation of the Crimea, in the autumn and winter of 1784–5, that he next went south. Finally, two years later he was sent ahead to prepare gardens at all Catherine's stopping-points during her famous imperial progress through New Russia. "Gould employed a staff of 'several hundred assistants' who travelled in Potemkin's wake. He planned and executed gardens in Astrakhan, Ekaterinoslav, Nikolaev and the Crimea, including on the estates on the lush Crimean coast at Artek, Massandra, and the site of the Alupka Palace".[2]

Loudon writes, in 1834, "Sir John Carr relates an anecdote on Gould's authority, which was confirmed to us, in 1813, by the present gardener, Call, his successor, and deserves a place here. 'In one of the prince's journeys to the Ukraine, Gould attended him with several hundred assistants, destined for operators, in laying out the grounds of Potemkin's residence in the Crimea. Wherever the prince halted, if only for a day, his travelling pavilion was erected, and surrounded by a garden in the English taste, composed of trees and shrubs, divided by gravel walks, and ornamented with seats and statues, all carried forward with the cavalcade'".[3]

The great visitation started on the icy morning of 7th January, 1787, when "fourteen carriages, 124 sledges (and forty reserves) set off from Tsarskoe Selo to the sound of cannon salutes. Five hundred and sixty horses awaited them at each post. Catherine's entourage of twenty-two consisted of her senior courtiers … and the ambassadors of France, Austria and England. All were wrapped in bearskins and sable bonnets. They were accompanied by hundreds of servants,

[1] Cross, *By the Banks of the Neva*, 1997, p. 275.
[2] Montefiore, *op. cit.*, p. 305.
[3] Loudon, *op. cit.*, p. 249.

10. Mid-nineteenth-century chromolithograph of the parade ground at Bakhchisaray.
By permission of the Alupka Palace Archive.

including twenty footmen, thirty washerwomen, silver polishers, apothecaries, doctors and blackamoors".[1] On 29 January, they all arrived at Kiev, where they had to remain until the ice on the Dnieper melted and travel by water became possible.

At last, after nearly three months of waiting, on 22 April 1787, cannon declared that the thaw had come, and the party was able to embark. "The seven imperial galleys of the Prince's sublime fleet were elegant, comfortable and majestic, painted in gold and scarlet on the outside, decorated in gold and silk inside, propelled and served by 3,000 oarsmen, crew and guards, and attended by over eighty other boats. Each had its own orchestra, always on deck ... the floating dining-hall could seat seventy. The dazzling, almost mythical, memory of this cruise remained with all its guests for the rest of their lives ... The Prince presented a perpetual spectacle along the riverside: as they set off to cannon salvoes and symphonies, small squadrons of Cossacks manoeuvred over the plains. Towns, villages, country houses and sometimes rustic huts were so

[1]   Montefiore, *op. cit.*, p. 354.

11. Bakhchisaray: tulips in flower outside the staircase to the Harem.
Photograph by Paul Barker, Country Life Archive.

wonderfully adorned and disguised with garlands of flowers and splendid architectural decorations that they seemed to be transformed before our eyes into superb cities, palaces suddenly sprang up and magically created gardens".[1] Not for nothing had William Gould preceded his master .

On 25 April, King Stanislas-Augustus of Poland, who had twenty years earlier been one of her lovers, travelling under his original name of Count Poniatowski (for kings of Poland were not supposed to leave the country) met the Empress at Kaniev, proposing a Russo-Polish alliance; but was constrained to depart, "broken-hearted and humiliated". As the Prince de Ligne concisely put it, the King "had been here for three months and spent three million to see the Empress for three hours".

[1]   *Ibid.*, pp. 363–9.

12 (above). Entrance to Bakhchisaray, from inside the Maidan.
Photograph by Terence Reeves-Smith.

Early in May, the Empress and her entourage were met by Archduke
Joseph II of Austria-Hungary, in incognito this time as Comte de Falkenstein, at
Kaidak. Unfortunately, however, the barges, including those bearing the cooks
and the kitchens, had all run aground thirty miles upstream. The principal
actors had rushed overland to meet him. "Necessity driving, Prince Potemkin
himself became the *chef-de-cuisine* ... Prince de Nassau, the kitchen-boy, and
Grand General Branicki, the pastry-maker ... the two Majesties had never been
so grandly and *badly* served but it was such fun that it was as good a dinner as it
was bad".[1]

At long last, the voyage was nearing its climax. First they visited Kherson,
where Catherine and Joseph on 15th May launched three warships from the
new shipyards. Then, having passed through the Perekop Lines at the entrance
to the Crimea, the party was greeted by 1,200 Tatar horsemen. They had
arrived.

[1]   *Ibid.*, pp. 368–9.

14 (above). Detail of the stone-carving by Alevisio Novi at the elaborate portal of the reception hall at Bakhchisaray. Alevisio has been tentatively identified as Aloisio ('Aleuitius' in English) di Montagnana from Milan; described in Italian records as a stone-cutter, or mason; but despite the doubts of some Russian scholars, he seems to have blossomed in Moscow into a fully-fledged architect.
Photograph: Terence Reeves-Smyth.

13 (opposite page). The oldest part of the palace at Bakhchisaray is the ceremonial portal through which ambassadors and other potentates were admitted to the palace audience-hall. The elaborately-carved stone-work of the doorcase is the work of Alevisio Novi, an Italian stranded here for a year in 1503–4, on his way to Moscow, where he was to build the Archangelsk Cathedral in the Kremlin, and then live on for another thirty years until, apparently, being killed when his home was blown up in the explosion of a nearby gunpowder store.
Photograph: Terence Reeves-Smyth.

15 (next page, above). A view inside the harem at Bakhchisaray, now part of the Tatar Museum.
Photograph: Terence Reeves-Smyth.

16 (next page, below). The summer House, or Garden Room, beyond the Divan Hall at Bakhchisaray, dates from the seventeenth century and is decorated with stained glass in geometric panels, carved woodwork, filigree painting, and – best of all – delightful views into the courtyard garden outside. The central fountain and pool are of marble.
Photograph: Terence Reeves-Smyth.

II: THE GARDEN PALACE OF BAKHCHISARAY

In 1786, an anonymous contributor to the *Annual Register* (thought to have been a British Captain P*; edited by the British chaplain in St Petersburg, Rev. William Tooke) wrote: "Bachtichi-Sarai, an extensive and wealthy city, lying in a vale between two high mountains, and surrounded by a number of gardens. From this circumstance it has its name; Bachtichi signifying, in the Tartarian language, a garden, and Sarai, a palace".[1] (The spellings, and transliterations, of the names of the palace, and of its rulers, are numerous and varied; but I am assured that the best usages, in 2002, are those I here employ, save where the text is in quotation marks.)

Loudon, in 1834, waxes lyrical:

> In some places the limestone rocks overhang the houses in a threatening attitude, and amongst them are gardens filled with fruit trees, over which rises the tall and graceful poplar ... The apartments of the seraglio were painted with borders of flowers, and fitted up with curious inlaid presses for female attire, and the requisites for the toilette; beneath them were cool halls for the summer heats, in which marble fountains continually played; but the falling water had a melancholy sound in the deserted chambers. The gardens were latticed, and neatly laid out in parterres of flowers, with trellis-work for vines. The other apartments of the palace consisted of halls of audience, with sleeping apartments for the attendants.
>
> The former were lofty, with lancet windows, filled with stained glass, high moresque chimney-pieces, mirrors with gilt frames, glass cases filled with artificial flowers, landscapes and hunting-scenes painted on the cornices, and divans covered with brocade. Taken as a whole, the palace of Bucktesrai is a most interesting specimen of Tartaric magnificence, and a most desirable residence.[2]

In 1503, the Khan Mengli-Geray had built himself a palace at Devletsaray, and a summer palace at Salachik, each only a few miles from Bakhchisaray; and took advantage of the passing presence of the North Italian architect Alevisio Novi. He has been identified by Italian scholars as Aloisio Lamberti di Montagnana, from Milan; but some Russian scholars doubt this, since the latter was described merely as 'taiapiera', or stone-cutter, and they find it hard to accept that a humble stone-mason could blossom into so accomplished an

[1]   *Annual Register*, 1786, p. 132.
[2]   Loudon, *op. cit.*, p. 255.

architect.[1] The Tsar Ivan III had sent for Italian craftsmen to assist in the rebuilding of the Kremlin, but, because of the outbreak of war between Moscow and Lithuania in 1500, they were unable to take the usual route through Poland; however, Alevisio Novi and his companions were detained in Moldavia. They were rescued by Mengli-Geray, who employed Alevisio Novi between June 1503 and September 1504 to build him the remarkably elegant and sophisticated Italianate doorcase which was subsequently removed and re-erected at Bakhchisaray, and is now the oldest (and perhaps the best) element in the palace.[2] It is made of eighteen blocks of intricately-carved local limestone; the lunette in the pediment is carved from a single block. Vlasiuk says "The doorway was conceived and built as the main entrance into the palace of an oriental despot. It commanded the little courtyard in which the envoys of various states awaited their reception. The luxurious ornamentation of the designs, which were cut out in white stone and painted, formed an extraordinarily decorative composition ... characterised by the union of the classical order principle, with oriental, emphatically carpet-style decoration".[3] The inscription in the doorcase is translated, not without grandiloquence, as recording "This magnificent entrance and this majestic door were erected at the command of the sultan of two continents and ruler of two seas, sultan, son of the sultan, Mengli-Geray, son of Haji-Geray." Alevisio Novi went on to build the Italianate Archangelsky cathedral in the Kremlin, and eleven other churches in various districts of Moscow.[4] He spent thirty years there, and is thought to have been killed when his house was destroyed by the explosion of a nearby gunpowder store.

The new palace at Bakhchisaray was built between 1530 and 1550 by one of Mengli-geray's successors; probably Adil-Sahib-Geray; but his architect is not known. It has been conjectured that a Persian named Omar was concerned in the design, but it seems more probable that he was a craftsman concerned with the stone-carving of the fountains, and perhaps other features of the palace. Current opinion in the Museum is that "Everything we know about the Palace proves that it was built by Tatar builders (perhaps helped also by Turks)".[5] Certainly, its design appears to owe much to the layout of the Seraglio in the Topkapi Saray in Istanbul, which is not far from being a contemporary building.

[1]   Portoghesi, *Dizionario Enciclopedico di Architettura e Urbanistica*, 1968, p. 86.
[2]   Ernst, 'The Khan's palace at Bakhchiseray ... and Alevisio the Younger', 1928 (pages unnumbered).
[3]   Vlasiuk, 1958, p. 102.
[4]   Ernst, *op. cit.*
[5]   Letter to the author from A Haiworonsky, 29 April 2002.

II: THE GARDEN PALACE OF BAKHCHISARAY

In 1453, the Sultan Mehmed II at long last, after years of struggle, had succeeded in taking Byzantium. "It was he who chose Seraglio Point for building the palace which is now the Topkapi Seray". But it was to be enlarged, and improved, over many years; first, by the formidable conjunction of Suleyman the Magnificent, and his incomparable architect, Sinan, during the middle years of the sixteenth century: and later, by successive generations of Osmanli Sultans. Sinan was "the architect of that Abode of Felicity, the Topkapi Saray, which under Suleyman became the Sultan's home and harem, as well as being the seat of government. This change was one more instigated by Roxelana [his wife], perhaps her most lasting achievement. For the rest of the dynasty, the harem was to remain an integral part of the Palace".[1]

No group of buildings known to me more closely resembles the Topkapi enclave than Bakhchisaray, albeit on a considerably smaller scale. This comes as no great surprise, given that the Khans of Tartary and the Sultans of the Sublime Porte were, in a sense, cousins, both lines claiming direct descent from Genghis Khan (in the case of the Gerays) or from his principal officers (in the case of the Osmanlis). It was for years widely believed that, had the Ottoman line failed, the Gerays would have been next in succession to the whole Ottoman Empire; but Seymour concluded that no such right existed, and that "the opinion took its rise in vulgar error". The Bakhchisaray complex still covers over four hectares (around 20 acres) but was originally far more extensive. The front entrance is over a bridge across the river Churuk-Su, and under an archway leading into the first and largest courtyard. As in Istanbul, the first court was originally a *maidan,* or parade ground, where troops could be exercised or reviewed. To the left, were shops and stalls open to the citizenry. Then, within the walls, the great Mosque, with its twin tall minarets, rebuilt in 1740 on the foundations of a much earlier basilical building. Then comes the Khans' cemetery, where no less than 56 members of the Geray dynasty lie buried, and the octagonal eighteenth-century mausoleum of the Princess Diliara-Biketch, commemorated in the Fountain of Tears: as Montefiore says, "Beside the khans' mosque, with its high minarets, stood the haunting, noble graveyard of the Giray dynasty: two octagonal rotunda were built around the mausoleums of khans in a field of intricately carved gravestones".[2] Beyond that, the extensive stabling for the khan's horses, with accommodation above for horsemen and grooms: and beyond that again, extensive horse-meadows and pastures.

To the right of the entrance courtyard lay the public rooms, arranged around an intricate series of courts and gardens. The principal rooms and courtyards in this part of the palace were: the khan's chancellery; the justice

[1]   Levey, *The World of Ottoman Art,* 1975, pp. 39, 70.
[2]   Montefiore, *op. cit.,* p. 372.

17. The Fountain of Tears, in the Fountain Court at Bakhchisaray; of 1764, masterpiece of the Persian sculptor Omar. It is so designed that one drop at a time trickles down into the pool at its foot. It is reputed to have been dedicated by the warlike Khan Krim-Guirey to the memory of his wife, the beautiful foreign Princess Diliara, who could not endure the life of the harem and so died young.

In 1824, Pushkin's famous poem, 'the Fountain of Bakhchisaray', was published in Moscow; it made him a small fortune and firmly established his reputation; he identified the captive with the Polish princess Mariya, and wrote of her in terms of Byronic romanticism. It is still one of the best-known poems in Russian; a rose is placed every day, so long as roses are in season, in the topmost of its ten carved basins in memory of Pushkin.

Photograph: Terence Reeves-Smyth.

18. The Golden Fountain at Bakhchisaray, carved in 1733 for Kaplan Giray. Of marble, with the ornament, including scrollwork and foliage, raised and gilded, it incorporates two carved inscriptions. The upper gives the Khan's name and the date; the lower one, a poetical quotation from the Koran: "And the Lord gave the young men in Paradise a pure liquid to drink".

Photograph: Terence Reeves-Smyth.

19 (opposite). The seventeenth-century cemetery at Bakhchisaray: Simon Sebag-Montefiore has aptly described it as "the haunting, noble graveyard of the Giray dynasty". No fewer than fifty-six members of the family are buried here, with their relatives, mistresses and courtiers.

Photograph: Terence Reeves-Smyth.

32

20. Carved marble Giray tomb in the cemetery at Bakhchisaray. These tombstones for the most part date from the fourteenth and fifteenth centuries AD, although a few appear to be older, brought here from other graveyards. They exhibit elements deriving from Persia, Central Asia, and Turkey, interwoven with Italian Renaissance motifs. The gravestones of men are topped by a turban; those of women by a flat cap.
Photograph: Terence Reeves-Smyth.

chamber; the fountain yard; and the small palace mosque built in 1741. Its principal ornaments are, apart from Alevisio Novi's Iron Doorway, the Golden Fountain built by Kaplan Geray in 1733, and the Fountain of Tears (celebrated in a very well-known poem by Pushkin, in whose memory a rose is still placed daily on the fountain), built in 1763 by Khan Krym-Geray. All these rooms were originally richly furnished and ornamented, but little has survived. "According to witnesses, the khan's seat [in the Justice Chamber] was draped with fine orange fabric with a gold crescent embroidered on the inner side of the chairback. On both sides, in a semi-circle, there were smaller chairs – or, more exactly, stools – upholstered like the khan's seat, while along the walls were divans draped with the same material ... This is the most extensive and the highest – with two rows of windows – room in the palace".[1]

[1]   Fadayeva and Sokolova, *Bakhchisaray i okrestnosti*, 2000, p. 37.

II: THE GARDEN PALACE OF BAKHCHISARAY

Behind and beyond these apartments of state, stood the Golden Study, the Summer Pavilion, the Coffee-room or (from its wall-paintings of the city) Constantinople room, the khan's washroom, the khan's heir's room, the barber's room, and the Bagnio. The smaller and more intimate rooms had tinted window-panes, and greenery growing around the windows. Behind these rooms again stood the Harem, of which only a few rooms survive, now used as a museum of Tatar arts, crafts, and furnishings; and the so-called Falcon Tower.

This is an octagonal building, which formed part of the architectural complex of the Persian Garden, which had formerly included a Winter Palace. "According to the legend, falcons trained for (the) Khan's hunting were kept here; also (the) Khan's wives were allowed to rise on the upper store(y) and observe through the trellis the colourful life of the Palace".[1]

Burden, who seems to have visited the palace in 1844, remarks, not without justice, that "the pleasure of a visit to Baktcheserai depends upon the frame of mind of the traveller. It is true there is something grotesque, irregular, and barbarous, about the whole; that the workmanship is rough, the joints ill-fitted, and the colouring what some would call gaudy; but there is at the same time originality in the design, vivid fancy in the colouring, and a sense of the picturesque in the grouping together of the parts".[2]

The whole palace complex was extensively damaged in the Russo-Turkish wars of 1736, 1738, and 1771: the first of these caused a serious fire. It was largely repaired or rebuilt, apparently in the 1740s, "for which purpose building materials, architects and painters were sent by the Porte from Constantinople".[3] By 1783, when Shagin-Geray finally surrendered the Crimea to Russia, the palace was in a sorry state.

---

[1] *Ibid.*, p. 204.
[2] Seymour, *Russia on the Black Sea and Sea of Azov*, 1855, p. 41.
[3] Fadayeva and Sokolova, *op. cit.*, p. 23.

III: PRINCE POTEMKIN; CHARLES CAMERON;
LADY CRAVEN

Almost immediately after his bloodless victory – for the Crimea had been acquired by dint of negotiation, not bloodshed – Prince Potemkin began planning the expedition to bring his mistress, the Empress Catherine, to inspect the new lands of South Russia which he had won for her. In 1783, he sent instructions to Lieutenant-General Ingelshtrom – "The khan's palace ... is, I hear falling into decay. I recommend your Excellency to put it into the state in which it was formerly, and to correct all that has been ruined, taking care that the taste with which it was all constructed be preserved.".[1] On 28 June 1784, i.e. in the following year, Potemkin again issued an order to repair the palace. Captain Tomashevsky, assisted by Ensign Bushkovsky, was appointed to carry out the work. "The duties of architect were carried out by a Greek, Yusuf Calvé; the workmen, carpenters, stone-masons, plasterers and free-lance labourers were drawn partly from Tatars, partly from Russians – the latter being mainly soldiers and prisoners. There was in essence every chance of preserving the 'taste' in which everything had been built, since among the population of Bakhchisaray and among the workmen drawn from the Tatars there were undoubtedly people who were well acquainted with the finish of the palace. The painters, however, it turns out, had been brought in from Nezhino and the paint had been bought in Kharkov ... The local paints were very different from those imported later. The work was carried out in the course of three years, and cost 8542 roubles, 37 kopecks".[2] Early in 1787, perhaps dissatisfied with progress, Potemkin appointed Captain de Ribas to replace Tomashevsky.

All this leaves wide open the vexed question of the part, if any, played in the restoration of Bakhchisaray by the Empress's favourite, the Scottish architect Charles Cameron. He was a remarkable figure. "Cameron's reputation as one of the leading British neo-classical architects and one of the greatest British artists ever to have worked abroad has rested on the romantic haze surrounding his character and achievement. The truth is slightly different. His private life verges on the dishonourable and his architectural achievement is

---

[1] Gerngross, 'The Palace of the Khans at Backchisaray', 1912, p. 10.
[2] *Ibid.*, pp. 10, 11.

36

more modest though not less interesting than is generally supposed. There are no buildings by him in Scotland. The designs for country houses in the Russian provinces seem not to have been executed. His surviving fully documented Russian works are several suites of rooms, a church and outbuildings at Tsarskoe Selo, the exterior, garden buildings and some of the interiors at Pavlovsk, and possibly some of the buildings at the Naval Dockyards".[1] Despite all this, he is one of the most important neo-classical architects and interior decorators of the late eighteenth century, on a par with the Adam brothers; his work, especially at Tsarskoe Selo, is of the very highest quality. But did he, or did he not, work at the Palace of Bakhchisaray?

His English biographer, Isabel Rae, states quite definitely that he was involved as "restorer of the Khan's palace at Bakhchisarai; his aim, to transform it into a suitable imperial residence, a commission for which Isaac Ware and Palladio had not prepared him ... Whether Cameron was fully occupied by this work at Bakhchisarai, or whether he was also engaged on some of the new buildings erected along the route for Catherine's overnight stops, there is no means of knowing. The only certainty is that, in addition, he did construct one triumphal arch".[2] Anderson, historian of Scotsmen in Russia, also says that Cameron was given the job of restoring the Khan's palace at Backchisaray: "He was given one year to complete the task, which he did".[3] Kuznetzov and Howard seem to agree.[4]

But more recent historians take a different view. Shvidkovsky, in his very authoritative work, reached the conclusion that Cameron had not been involved; and that later researchers had been led to misunderstand the relationship between Cameron and his assistant, William Hastie, who was certainly involved (see below) a few years later.[5] And Cross says that "There is absolutely no evidence that Cameron ever went to the Crimea. I came to that conclusion independently of my friend Shvidkovsky".[6]

Whoever were the authors of this notable restoration, they appear to have given satisfaction.

Lady Elizabeth Craven, in 1786, was (why?) privileged not only to have a preview of the accommodation prepared for the Empress, but also to occupy it herself. On 3 March, 1786, she wrote: "The Khan's palaces, noble Tartar houses, and others are prepared for her reception, in which I am assured I shall be

---

[1] Rae, *Charles Cameron*, 1971, p. 63.
[2] *Ibid.*
[3] Anderson, *Scotsmen in the Service of the Czars*, 1990, p. 160.
[4] Howard and Kuznetsov, 'Scottish Architecture in Czarist Russia', 1996, pp. 35–41.
[5] Shvidkovsky, 1996, *op. cit.*, p. 238.
[6] Letter to the author from Professor Cross, 27 August 2002.

received and treated perfectly well".[1] Was this perhaps some kind of a practice run, organised by Potemkin? Her letters were best-sellers, "Not that by nature the beautiful Lady Craven was ever discreet or free from the attentions of the then 'tabloid press': long parted from her husband, after being caught *in flagrante* with the French ambassador to the Court of St James's, she embarked on her travels with Henry Vernon, a grand nephew of Admiral Vernon, while writing letters to her 'brother', the Margrave [of Anspach] whom she was to marry in 1791".[2]

In her Letter XLI, dated from Bakhchisaray, April 3 1786, Lady Craven writes: "Batcheserai is situated in so steep a valley, that some of the hanging pieces of rock seem ready to fall and crush the houses ... There are five thousand Tartar inhabitants here ... There is a great trade here of blades and swords, hangers, and knifes ... I am assured many made here are not to be distinguished from those of Damascus – The Khan's palace is an irregular building, the greatest part of it is one floor raised upon pillars of wood painted and gilt in a fanciful and lively manner, the arch, or last door-way, has fine proportions, a large inscription in gilt letters is the chief ornament – I am told it was perfectly in ruins, but the governor has had it repaired, new gilt and painted for the Empress's reception. Court within court, and garden within garden, make a variety of apartments where the Khan walked from his own residence to the Harem, which is spacious and higher than the other buildings – What I thought pretty enough was that several of the square places under his apartment were paved with marble, and have in the center fountains which play constantly. My room is a square of more than forty feet, having two rows of windows one above the other on three sides, and it was with difficulty I found a place to have my bed put up in – I never saw such a variety of colours – different coloured gold and silver mixed together. The Kaima-Kan, and two other principal Tartars, supped with us, and I find nothing can exceed the ignorance, and simplicity of these people. The Kaima-Kan is the Khan's first minister; he is totally ignorant of the geography of his own country; and says that England and Petersburgh are the same thing ... I saw from the windows a kind of dome which raised my curiosity, and I am told it is a monument built to the memory of a Christian wife, which the Khan loved so tenderly that he was inconsolable for her loss; and that he had placed it there, that he might have the satisfaction of looking at the building which contained her remains. Many buildings, such as baths, summer-houses, &c., are in ruins near Batcheserai. I went into one bath, it was circular, having white marble on the inside, with niches for the bathers to sit in, which we have no idea of. Cold bathing is unknown in Turkey and Tartary ... *P.S.* Wild asparagus grows in great plenty all over the peninsula, and a

---

[1]   Craven, *op. cit.*, 1814, p. 202.
[2]   Cross, *By the Banks of the Neva*, 1997, pp. 358–9.

wild kind of horse-radish of an enormous size, and the strongest and best flavoured I ever tasted, the root is as long and as big as the stoutest leg you ever saw".[1]

In August, 1793, another visitor from England recorded his impressions of the palace: Rev. John Parkinson, acting as bear-leader to a young Englishman engaged on an unusually northern version of the Grand Tour. They both stayed there as guests of Admiral Mordvinov and his English wife, who had made it their official residence, comparatively far as it was from the sea. "The apartments which the Admiral made use of consisted of several small ones and were thrown into their present form against the Empress's coming. In those which we occupy, and which were the Audience Chambers of the Khan, the Empress also gave Audience ... We dined in a large lofty room on the ground floor which served in the Khan's time for the state audience chamber. Our own quarters are his other state rooms, and that part of the Palace which Admiral and Madame Mordvinoff inhabit were his private apartments. When the Empress was here she put them all to their proper use. In order to come to [the Harem] it was necessary to pass through the apartment of the chief Eunuch ... and he took care that no improper person should go that way". Parkinson's journal includes a plan of the palace, and a very detailed description of the Audience Chamber: "the large O is the Chimney, which has so much the appearance of a seat or throne that Bootle [his protégé] actually asked whether the Khan did not sit there ... NB In these apartments one hears the fountain in the Hall below and they have at least at this time of the year a most charming effect. It would have been thought a great rudeness for anyone to come upon [the Divan] with his slippers on ... We found in our apartment the table which the Khan made use [of] to dine: it was about a foot and a half high and the same in width: the materials wood painted. They have only one dish set on at a time and use neither Knives nor Forks". The party stayed for four days, and greatly enjoyed their visit. "From the windows of our apartment on the left we see a part of the town situated at the foot of a high mountain which puts out rocks in several places in a singular way; on the right we have the Khan's Garden, a Mausoleum built in honour of some favourite relation, a Tartar burial ground consisting of a large garden and a high hill by way of termination to the whole: in front are the mosque and two mausoleums which served as places of interment to the Royal Family: over these the most romantic part of the rocks present themselves".[2]

[1]   Craven, *op. cit.*, pp. 233–239.
[2]   Parkinson, *A Tour of Russia, Siberia and the Crimea, 1792–1794*, 1971, pp. 193–198.

IV: THE IMPERIAL VISITATION

"After Kherson, the two Caesars headed across the bare steppe towards the Crimea ... Suddenly, the imperial carriage was surrounded by 3,000 Don Cossacks in full regalia, led by their ataman, in a single row, ready to charge ... At dusk, Joseph and Ségur walked out into the flat, apparently endless wasteland, nothing but grass all the way to the horizon. 'What a peculiar land,' said the Holy Roman Emperor. 'And who could have expected to see me with Catherine the Second and the French and English ambassadors wandering through a Tartar desert? What a page of history!'."[1]

As the party crossed the Perekop line into the Crimea, they were greeted by 1,200 Tatar cavalrymen, armed with jewelled pistols, curved daggers, lances, and bows and arrows, "as if the travellers had suddenly passed backwards into Europe's dark past".[2] There was nearly an accident as they drove down the steep ravine leading to Bakhchisaray: the horses bolted, throwing Catherine's and Joseph's carriage off the hill, between dangerous rocks. But the escort of Tatars managed to halt the runaway: and Catherine displayed no fear.

"The Khan's Palace was an eclectic compound of palace, harem and mosque ... its courtyards were silent and serene. Towering walls surrounded secret gardens, soothed by the trickle of elaborate fountains ... Sweet scents rose from burning candles beneath the windows. Around the Palace stood a Tartar town with its baths and minarets, in a valley wedged between two sheer cliffs of rock. Potemkin had covered these with burning lanterns so that the travellers really felt that they resided in a mythical Arabian palace in the middle of an illuminated amphitheatre".[3]

"An inscription on the pillar of the front gate states that 'The Empress Catherine II was pleased to visit Bakhchisaray on 14 May 1787'. Unfortunately [says Gerngross], none of her travelling companions left anything like a colourful description of the palace, though almost all of them have written their memoirs".

The inner core of this extraordinary house-party now consisted of, naturally, the Empress, fifty-eight years old and still in her prime; Joseph II, aged forty-six, Holy Roman Emperor; Prince Potemkin, then forty-eight; the

---

[1] Montefiore, *op. cit.*, p. 371.
[2] *Ibid.*, p. 371.
[3] *Ibid.*, p. 372.

French ambassador, Louis-Philippe, Comte de Ségur: "Round-faced, with his eyebrows always raised, and a permanently amused expression like a smiling marmoset ... aged thirty-two ... an ornament to the epoch which he recorded so elegantly in his *Mémoires*. Son of a French marshal and war minister, friends with Marie-Antoinette, Diderot and d'Alembert, and a veteran of the American War";[1] the Prince de Ligne, aged fifty-two, "the intimate friend and counsellor of the emperor Joseph II",[2] born in Brabant, a distinguished Austrian warrior, eventually field-marshal both in the Austrian and Russian armies – "affectionate with his equals, popular with his inferiors, familiar with princes and even sovereigns, he put everyone at their ease";[3] and, though rather more reserved and withdrawn, the English Envoy Extraordinary, Alleyne Fitzherbert, a professional diplomat aged only thirty-four, later to negotiate the peace treaty between Britain and Russia of 1801, for which he was raised to the peerage: "a man of consummate prudence and quiet, polished manners". Fitzherbert's "conversation was always attractive, and amongst his best stories were his anecdotes of the empress and her court".[4]

To these, of course, must be added Russian courtiers and court officials. But it seems clear that, on the whole, though it had its serious aspects, and despite the disparate ages of the participants, this must have been an extremely jolly and indeed amusing party. Ligne, in his old age, was to be the author of the well-known witticism, of the Congress of Vienna, "Le Congrès danse, mais il ne marche pas".

Catherine stayed in the rooms of the Khan, including the audience chamber; the Kaiser stayed in the rooms of the Khan's heir; Potemkin and Ligne (not inappropriately) stayed in the Harem. Ligne and Catherine were "captivated by the magic of the place. The delicious sweet scents of the gardens – orange trees, roses, jasmine, pomegranates – pervaded every apartment, each of which had a divan round its walls and a fountain in the middle. At Catherine's dinners, she received the local muftis, whom she treated respectfully. She was inspired by the imams calling the faithful to prayer five times a day".[5] Yet they only stayed, in the first instance, for two nights.

Their first, and principal, stop was at a pretty palace on the Heights of Inkerman overlooking the inlet of Sevastopol. Here they viewed for the first time Potemkin's brand-new Black Sea fleet, no fewer than twenty battleships and frigates, all built within the previous two years. At a signal from Potemkin, all the ships fired a salvo by way of salute. "Madam", said Ségur, "by creating

[1] *Ibid*., p. 322.

[2] *Encyclopaedia Britannica*, 11th edn, XVI, p. 679.

[3] Montefiore, *op. cit.*, p. 357.

[4] *Dictionary of National Biography*, XVI, 1889, pp. 166–7.

[5] Montefiore, *op. cit.*, pp. 372–3.

Sebastopol, you have finished in the South what Peter the Great began in the north".[1] Then they were rowed round the fleet, to land at the new admiralty building of the port.

On the following days, the party went sight-seeing along the southern coastal strip of the Crimea, between the sea and the mountains. They then turned inland to inspect "Potemkin's gardens, dairies, flocks of sheep and goats, and his pink 'Tartar' palace at Karasubazaar ... They found an English island here. Capability Brown would have recognised the English gardens –'clumps of majestic trees, a most extensive lawn', leading to 'woods which would make a delightful pleasure ground laid out by our countryman Gould' and there was Henderson's English dairy. Potemkin's idyll was incomplete without a full English tea, too".[2] Then the party returned to Bakhchisaray, before it finally broke up on the steppes of Kizikerman on 2 June, when Catherine headed north in the direction of Moscow, Joseph westward towards Vienna. The Empress finally arrived back at Tsarskoe Selo on 22 July, after an absence from St Petersburg of just over six months.

The whole trip had been a triumph, especially for its sponsor and organiser, Potemkin. The Empress, who always enjoyed and took an interest in the customs and manners of her more exotic subjects, was fascinated in particular by the Cossacks, and the Tatars. She gave directions that the palace of Bakhchisaray should be kept in good repair, and that its Oriental character should be maintained or, where necessary, restored. These instructions were eventually, after her death in 1796, to lead to the drawings prepared by the Scotsman, William Hastie, for Potemkin's successor as Governor of Taurida and at the same time Catherine's last lover, Platon Zubov.

[1]   *Ibid.*, p. 373.
[2]   *Ibid.*, pp. 377–8.

V: THE AFTERMATH OF THE VISITATION:
WILLIAM HASTIE

In August, 1779, Charles Cameron set sail from London for his new life in St Petersburg. From 1780 until 1795 he was involved in work at Tsarskoe Selo; but by 1784 he had become deeply dissatisfied with the skills of the Russian craftsmen, who had been more accustomed to working with axes, adzes or hatchets on timber rather than with stone. In January 1784 he took the extreme step, on his own account and without authorisation, of advertising in the *Edinburgh Evening Courant* as follows:[1]

> For her Majefty the Emprefs of all the Ruffias.
> WANTED,
> TWO CLERKS, who have been employed by an Architect or very confiderable Builder, who can draw well, fuch as figures and ornaments for rooms, &c. &c.
>   Two Mafter Mafons,
>   Two Mafter Bricklayers,
>   A Mafter Smith, who can make locks, hinges, &c.
>   Several Journeymen Plafterers,
>   Several Journeymen Bricklayers.
>   It is expected that none will apply who are not fully mafters of the above work, and who cannot bring with them proper certificates of their abilities and good behaviour.
>   The mafter mafons, bricklayers, and fmith, muft have been employed as foremen in their different lines. The mafter bricklayers and men will have a pice of ground given them. As the encouragement to each will be confiderable, the beft of tradefmen will be expected.
>   For further particulars apply to Meffrs Peter and Francis Forrefter and Company, Leith, who will have a good veffel ready to carry them out by the 1ft of April next, provided the Baltic is by that time open.

Seventy-three experienced men were engaged. In May they set off in the ship *Betsey and Brothers,* many of them bringing with them their wives and children, a party of some 140 persons in all. Professor Cross has established that the group included twenty-seven stonemasons, fifteen bricklayers, fifteen plasterers, and five blacksmiths. They were greeted at Kronstadt by Cameron himself.[2] Their arrival caused some consternation amongst the English, for it was against Government policy to allow skilled craftsmen to go abroad. This

[1]   *Edinburgh Evening Courant*, 21 January 1784. Reproduction courtesy of the National Library of Scotland, Edinburgh.
[2]   Cross, 'Charles Cameron's Scottish workmen', 1988.

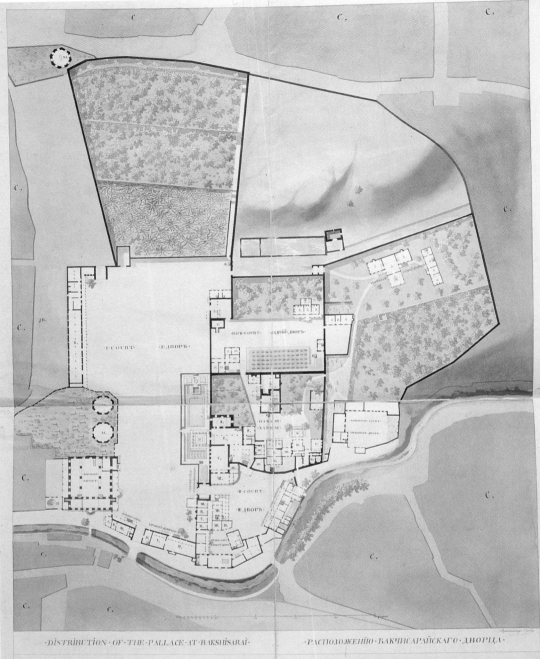

DISTRIBUTION·OF·THE·PALLACE·AT·BAKSHISARAÏ. ·РАСПОЛОЖЕНIЮ·БАКЧИСАРАЙСКАГО·ДВОРЦА.

22 (opposite). The Ground Plan of 'The Pallace of Bakhchisaray', drawn and coloured by William Hastie in 1798, from the Album, now in the National Library of Russia, St Petersburg, presented to Catherine the Great's successor, Tsar Paul I.

23 (next two pages, above). Elevation of the principal front of the palace of Bakhchisaray, seen from the exterior, by William Hastie, 1798. To the left the mosque, the entrance to the great courtyard, the buildings of the palace proper, and the Falcon Tower in the background.

24 (next two pages, below). The interior of the principal courtyard, by William Hastie: from the left, the mosque, the Geray mausolea and graveyard and the wooden stable block.

All three photographs courtesy of National Library of Russia, MS F. XIII.6

large party of Scots was accommodated in a specially-built so-called 'English Village' at Tsarskoe Selo. Some of them stayed for the year initially contracted for; some stayed longer; a few, including both Cameron and Hastie, never came home to Scotland at all, except perhaps for short visits.

Amongst those on board was William Hastie (known in Russia as Viliam Gesti), one of the junior stone-masons. Little is known of his background or previous life; though he seems to have been born in about 1755, and if so was 32 when he sailed to Russia. Cross believes that "he developed his skills as a draughtsman while working in Cameron's design team". Certainly he was, or was to become, a highly accomplished draughtsman. He worked closely with Cameron, "and may even have been one of his design assistants ... While there is no documentary evidence to illuminate his personality, the evidence of his career indicates a highly intelligent young man, very capable of learning, who repeatedly used his initiative to expand his professional opportunities".[1]

Hastie was taken into Catherine's private service in 1792, and a couple of years later she told Baron Grimm that "Ce Hastie, architecte, dont vous me parlez, je l'ai pris à mon service; c'est un sujet très recommandable: il a fait des choses charmantes". In 1795 he married Margaret Bryce, daughter of one of his fellow masons. In the same year, he was fortunate enough to be appointed chief architect to Count Platon Zubov, then Governor of Ekaterinoslav and Taurida. "Zubov was almost the only person in Russia who could commission an architect serving in the imperial inner circle for any other task".[2] Hastie was to remain in the Crimea for four years.

In 1798, Hastie made measured drawings of the palace at Bakhchisaray with a view to its repair and restoration, "contained in an album of thirty-four sheets in the Saltikov-Tsedrin Library and which have remained of great importance to this day ... Hastie's designs are beautifully drawn and highly professional with

[1] Cross, *By the Banks of the Neva*, 1997, p. 305.
[2] Shvidkovsky, 1996, *op. cit.*, p. 238.

·ENTRANCE·FRONT·

·ELEVATION·OF·THE·MOSQUE·MAUSOLEUMS·AN

· ПЕРЕДНІЙ · ФАСАДЪ ·

· ФАСАДЪ · ГРОБНИЦЪ · МЕЧЕТИ · И · КОНЮШНИ ·

Elevation of the upper Mausoleum. *фасадъ верхней Гробницы.*

25. The Geray dynasty's graveyard, and the Upper Mausoleum, delineated by William Hastie in 1798. The building is not much changed today.

Photograph courtesy of the National Library of Russia, St Petersburg, MS F. XIII.6.

outlines and wash of exceptional delicacy".[1] Several of them were engraved, and the prints of these have survived in the palace archive. By far the most important is a ground plan of the entire complex, with a legend (both in Russian and in English) not only identifying the principal buildings, but actually giving brief details of their materials and condition in 1798.

For example: "In the Center-Pile: I Hall of Stone, Walls plaistered, Pillars and Ceiling of wood painted; II Mosque arched with Stone, Walls and Ceiling plaistered and painted; III Divan with marble floor and fountain – the walls and ceiling painted and gilt; IV The Walls and Ceilings plaistered; V Audience hall, the floor of Stone, Ceiling wood, of wood painted and gilt; VI, VII, VIII, IX, X, XI, XII, XIII, XIV, to XV. The walls plaistered, Ceilings boarded and painted". And: "In the left wing: the Rooms are finished with plaister and the Coridor on the front with blinds of network between the pillars". And: "Mosque, the Walls plaistered, Ceiling of wood painted; Mausoleums, of cut Stone the domes covered with lead". And "The Stables: finished in a bad stile; in the Bakehouse Court, it is all finished in a bad stile". Cisterns are separately marked 'A', Fountains 'B', and 'C', "Part of the Town".

[1]   Korshunova, 'William Hastie in Russia', 1974.

V: THE AFTERMATH OF THE VISITATION: WILLIAM HASTIE

Other engravings show the Principal Elevation of the entire complex, and Elevations of the Tombs, Mosque and Stables; of the Harem; of the Mausolea; and of the Fountain Court. Although Hastie produced panoramic views and measured drawings of a considerable number of other towns and buildings in the Crimea, there seems to be no evidence that he ever actually involved himself in conservation work, either at Bakhchisaray or elsewhere. He returned to St Petersburg in June 1799, and following the accession of the Tsar Alexander I, carved out for himself a completely new career as an engineer, a specialist in bridges, particularly of cast iron. Cross speculates that his association with Charles Gascoigne, and his assistant Alexander Wilson, son of one of the smiths who had travelled from Scotland in 1784, may well have given him a knowledge of the latest techniques in cast-iron bridge building developed in England and Germany in the 1790s. In the event, he was to be responsible for a considerable number of new bridges over the river Moyka and the canals of St Petersburg, of which only one survives. In 1817, he was awarded a 'princely' state pension of 1,500 roubles per annum, specifically for his bridge work.[1]

Finally, he was to establish himself in yet another new career: "Hastie's renown as a builder of bridges was rivalled and indeed eclipsed by his sudden reputation as a planner of towns ... In 1809 he and the Italian architect Luigi Rusca produced an album of standardised façades for private two- and three-storeyed houses in towns throughout Russia ... he produced in 1811 a series of twenty-six plans for standardised town areas or quarters, and squares ... Full layouts of towns were the peak of his planning and regulating activities ... for nearly twenty years, nearly up to his death in 1832, he was the empire's master planner". Although his proposals were not adopted in full, he played a major part in the rebuilding of Moscow in 1812 after the great firing of the city. Of the forty-seven squares he planned, twenty-six were realised, despite formidable difficulties arising from the claims of those who had title to the land, as were the rings of main roads. In 1819 he was accorded the high honour of Collegiate Assessor. As Shvidkovsky says, "Hastie's huge contribution to the development of Russian towns is indisputable. Many of them still retain features of his planning".[2] Unfortunately, there appears to be no known likeness of William Hastie, not even a sketch or caricature.

In June, 1799, Hastie had returned to St Petersburg. His drawings of Bakhchisaray were sent to the State Treasurer, approved, and substantial sums were allocated for its repair and for its future upkeep, and money was certainly spent, mainly on repairs to floors, ceilings and woodwork. In 1818, the Tsar Alexander I visited the palace, but no further repairs had then been carried out, and it was only in 1820 that the task of overall restoration was confided to the

[1] Shvidkovsky, 1996, *op. cit.*, pp. 239–40.
[2] Shvidkovsky, 1996, *op. cit.*, p. 251.

architect Kolodin, who had been sent south to Simferopol by the Ministry of Internal Affairs. By then, the palace was in a lamentable condition generally, worst of all being the Harem. In 1821, the Tsar approved the "sound improvement" of the palace, and a special committee was set up to supervise Kolodin and his work. But either the committee, or Kolodin, or both, proved incompetent, despite having employed a Greek, Michael Klado (incidentally, a British citizen) described as being "a well-known master craftsman in Asiatic work".[1]

Eugène Pascal, a pupil of Percier and Fontaine, next reported that "The palace of Bakhchisaray is in a most terrible state and the changes now being undertaken would be useless, as all the floors and corners are in the highest degree of dilapidation and the repair work every day reveals new shortcomings; the rooms and staircases are in places held up by continually renewed supports, which is very ugly. It is dangerous to leave the pavilion, as it may collapse; the trellis in the little garden has rotted and the fountains need the most detailed correction. The architect who has been sent by the Governor [evidently Kolodin] has drawn up plans for the palace and has given the project a European architectural character; but in my opinion it is necessary to restore it in its present form, as otherwise the aim of preserving this monument of Asiatic grandeur will not be achieved". Another Committee soon after wrote, "the wish of the Sovereign Emperor that the palace should be rebuilt in Asiatic taste has not been carried out, for many parts of it are being erected in complete accordance with European architecture; all the decorations, both interior and exterior, are ugly and not done in oriental taste".[2]

In consequence, the new Governor, Count Vorontsov, went in person to see for himself in July 1824: and the next month appointed a commission of inquiry. It reported that there had been many irregularities, both architectural and financial: and the services of Kolodin were forthwith dispensed with. Vorontsov appointed Philip Elson as architect in his place: and the latter was to spend the next six years on a painstaking restoration of Bakhchisaray.

[1] Gerngross, *op. cit.*, p. 25.
[2] *Ibid.*, p. 26.

VI: PHILIP ELSON AT BAKHCHISARAY

Philip Elson – otherwise, in Russian, Filipp Fyodorovich Elson; on his gravestone in Paris, Philippe d'Elson – was born in 1785, according to his gravestone, though later dates have been suggested. Palchikova says "Though in origin an Englishman, he had spent his whole life in Russia".[1] His Englishness, however, is not altogether free from doubt. The patronymic would seem to indicate that his father's Christian name was Theodore; but I have failed to discover amongst peerage, baronetage, or knightage, any plausible candidate who was in St Petersburg at the appropriate date. And, by coincidence or otherwise, his education (and that of his artist brother, Ivan) was paid for by a certain Baron, later Graf, Johann Martin Elmpt. Is it by chance that both names begin with "El"? Why should a stranger pay for the boys' education? On the other hand, it was only in 1796 that Elmpt was appointed to command the St Petersburg Grenadier Regiment. Yet again, it is by no means impossible that his service in the Russian army in Courland, Livonia, and the Baltic wars should have brought him to the capital on earlier dates.[2] And, still again, it was sometimes Russian practice to drop the first syllable of the father's name for a bastard: for example, I. I. Betskoi, secretary to Catherine the Great, was an illegitimate son of Prince Trubetskoi. So, Michaelson, Mendelson – or even perhaps Mandelson? – might have been the father's name. The truth of Elson's parentage may never be established: but for the purposes of this piece, I have elected to take his English origin at face value. And it seems plain that he was one of the earliest specialised conservation architects in Europe: earlier than Prosper Mérimée or Viollet-le-Duc in France; John Ruskin or William Morris in England.

He entered the Academy of Arts in St Petersburg, at a quite early age, in 1799. He proved a diligent student, winning a number of silver and gold medals. In 1810 he was called upon to design "a cathedral church to hold up to 10,000 persons ... a separate bell-tower ... a diocesan home to house the bishop and all the clergy, a house for the consistory and buildings for a seminary for 300 persons ... and to provide houses separately for the citizens".[3] This quite

---

[1]   Palchikova, 'F. F. Elson', 1997, p. 185.
[2]   *Deutschbaltisches Biographisches Lexicon*, 1970, p. 186.
[3]   Serbov, 'F. F. Elson', in *Russian Biographical Dictionary* (reprint 1962), XXIV, pp. 222–3.

extraordinarily exacting task he performed with success, gaining a large gold medal and the right to travel abroad at state expense.

He seems to have spent the next six years in Italy, pursuing his studies, partly at the expense of the Countess Potocka, for whom he was later to build a house at Livadia, and to have been admitted to the Academies both of Rome and of Florence. He returned to Russia in 1824; as early as 1818, the Tsar Alexander I presented him with a diamond ring as a reward for his design for a ballroom.[1] In the year of his return he was sent south as first holder of the newly-created post of Chief Architect for the South Coast, under the new Governor, Count Vorontsov, at a salary of 2,000 roubles per annum.

His principal task was to be the restoration of the Palace of Bakhchisaray: and the remedying, so far as possible, of the disastrous mistakes made by his predecessor Kolodin. No detailed record of his work seems to have survived; it is plain that he made good use of Hastie's drawings, though the destruction of the Harem in particular had progressed beyond all possibility of recreation. "Elson showed himself to be a serious and capable architect. He made a thorough study of the architecture of the palace, ... and in accordance with the general character of the site put together a plan for further repairs which was endorsed by the emperor. Almost everything which had been done by Kolodin himself had to be rebuilt *ab initio*. In this connection a very big repair and restoration programme was carried through. In 1825 Alexander I came to Bakhchisaray and was satisfied with the restoration work. But it was only in December 1831 that the palace was put into commission following the repairs".[2] The cost of the restoration, over the period of six years, amounted to 188,188 roubles.

In June of 1834, the restored palace was visited by a party of notables, comprising Count Vorontsov, his former enemy (now friend) the exiled Duc de Raguse (formerly Maréchal de Marmont), Prince Michael Galitzin, M. Bosmakoff, marshall of the Russian nobility, and a Doctor Seng. Marmont described Bakhchisaray in some detail, remarking appreciatively "On l'a réparé avec soin; il est bien entretenu, et présente le même aspect que lorsqu'il était habité".[3]

There can be no doubt that, despite numerous more recent restorations, the present admirable state of the palace is due principally to the combined efforts of William Hastie and Philip Elson. Nicholas I visited the palace in 1837; and in 1845, the Grand Prince Konstantin; and on each occasion there was a flurry of refurbishment. It seems to have been used on occasions to house important visitors: Kohl, in 1842, wrote "The former palace of the Khans has

[1] Palchikova, *op. cit.*, p. 186.
[2] *Ibid.*
[3] Raguse, Duc de, *Voyage*, I, p. 290.

been not only repaired, but even restored by the Russian government, and some of the apartments are beautifully fitted up in the oriental taste, for the reception of distinguished guests ... Food, attendance and so forth, one must of course find for one's self ... The outside of the palace is by no means striking, as it is surrounded by a high wall, and has the appearance of being a convent, but the interior is very pretty, with airy courts and gardens, terraces, and cool splashing fountains, and flower beds that fill the air with fragrance".[1]

During the Crimean War, the building was for almost two years used as a military hospital. This did the palace little good. According to Gerngross, one N. Berg, in his campaign notes, remarked "The palace has suddenly aged by 50 years. The Moorish mats have disappeared, as have the marble tables, the cunningly-crafted painted mirrors, the china candlesticks, the crystal chandeliers and the khans' wives' wardrobe ... The watchman Augustus has collected this and that in one of the rooms. From a pool full of water he will carefully drag out for you a glass chandelier which he is trying to wash clean. He will open a cupboard and show you some of the khans' candlesticks. He will array himself before you in the khan's brocade shawl which used to be hung about the last Girey when his head was being shaved".[2]

A number of repairs were carried out during the second half of the nineteenth century; on 17 July, 1892, "a terrible storm broke out over Backchisaray, from which the palace suffered severely".[3] It seems that one more campaign of restoration was carried out before the Revolution. The palace is now a well-preserved, well-presented, and much-visited museum.

As will be seen, Vorontsov did not directly employ Elson on his Alupka palace; although he worked on a number of subsidiary buildings, and on quite important buildings at Simferopol and elsewhere in the Crimea. But, it appears – perhaps on account of an unfortunate experience at Odessa – that the Count preferred to keep the construction of his favourite palace entirely in the hands of native Englishmen.

---

[1] Kohl, *Russia*, 1842, p. 460.
[2] Gerngross, *op. cit.*, p. 27.
[3] *Ibid.*, p. 28.

To the Magistrates Noblemen and Gentlemen of Cheshire this Portrait of
Thomas Harrison Esq.r to whose Taste the County is indebted for its Princi.
Architectural Embellishments is inscribed by their humble Serv.t A.R Burt
Miniature Painter Chester May 1 18..

26. Thomas Harrison of Chester, architect (1744–1829), "a plain man in person and manners, with an embarassed delivery in conversation, but very clear and ready in explaining with his pencil" (Joseph Farrington, 1795). His practice lay exclusively in the north of England; had it not done so, he would certainly have been better known, for he had 'the spark divine'. The two Counts Vorontsov, father and son, admired his work.

Etching of 1824 after Albin Roberts Burt, Chester Community History and Heritage.

VII: THOMAS HARRISON OF CHESTER
AND COUNT VORONTSOV

Thomas Harrison, of Chester (1744–1829), was well thought of in his own lifetime and beyond. Colvin says he "enjoyed a high reputation among contemporary architects. 'Harrison,' wrote C. R. Cockerell in 1823, 'has a spark divine.' Almost, if not quite, the first architectural genius of the kingdom' was the verdict of his first biographer ... Only his isolation in Chester and a natural diffidence prevented him from becoming a national figure like Soane or Smirke". He was best known for his bridges, and his public buildings; these included the Shire Hall, Grand Jury Room, and Gaol, in the reconstructed Lancaster Castle; the County Courts, Prison, Armoury, Barracks Exchequer and Gateway in Chester Castle; the Grosvenor Bridge at Chester; and significant public buildings in Liverpool and Manchester. "His Chester Castle complex forms the finest group of Greek Revival buildings in Britain – the neo-classical counterpart of Chelsea Hospital".[1]

However, his contribution to domestic architecture represented a small but nonetheless important part of his output. Between 1790 and 1820, some twelve villas were completed to his designs. Early on, at Kennet House, in Clackmannanshire, he established a successful formula in ashlar, with segmental projections, tripartite windows, simple consoles: and, in order to avoid fuss, the omission of window-sills. His first seven houses were all in various degrees refinements of this style: the last, Woodbank, at Stockport had recessed corners giving an effect of considerable subtlety – "a combination of Greek Revival style with a thoroughly convenient interior" (Ockrim). Thereafter, he gracefully abandoned ashlar in favour of the growing Regency vogue for brick walls encased in lined and painted stucco. His last stucco villa, and some consider his most successful, he built for his own occupation on the outskirts of Chester, at St Martin's Lodge: it was visited, and praised, by Cockerell in 1823.

According to his obituary in the *Gentleman's Magazine* of 1829, "Several years since Mr. Harrison was honoured with a visit from Count Woronzow, formerly Ambassador from the Court of Russia to England, who was passing through Chester, and expressed much admiration of the county hall, gaol, and other buildings at the Castle; and, six or seven years since, he was requested by

---

[1] Colvin, *Biographical Dictionary*, 1995, p. 46.

the son of the above, Count Michael Woronzow, to design a palace to be built in the Ukraine, upon the banks of the Dnieper ... and the Count came to Chester several times to see and consult with him ... This design, which was approved of by Count Woronzow, is in the Grecian style ... A tower or lighthouse more than 100 feet in height, for which Mr Harrison made a design, has been built by Count Woronzov upon an eminence from whence it may be seen from the Black Sea".[1] Colvin bases his account of Harrison's work in Russia on this obituary, and on the surviving drawings in the archive at Chester. But, there seems to have been some confusion here.

First, there seems never have been such a Greek Revival palace on the banks of the Dnieper as here referred to: though there may well have been projects for such a palace. Second, it is clear that Harrison did provide Vorontsov with designs for a Greek Revival official residence in Odessa; and that these were carried out, but that the design was altered and botched by the executant architect, the local Francesco Boffo. The opinions of critics seem to be unfavourable to this design: the building still stands. Third, the tower did indeed exist, at Moshny, near Cherkassy, in Kiev province, but far from the Black Sea: where the Vorontsov-Branitsky family had another, inland, estate. It seems to have been very similar to the Jubilee Tower on Moel Famma, in North Wales, erected by Harrison to celebrate the silver jubilee of George III; illustrated in the Chester exhibition of Harrison's work;[2] there is quite a good photograph of the Moshny tower in the Alupka archive, of 1915; it is said to have had 167 steps, and to have been a landmark for miles around. Used as an observation post in the 1940s, it was consequently destroyed by artillery fire.[3] However, despite these discrepancies, it does seem almost certain that Harrison, notwithstanding his advanced age, was responsible for the initial design of the palace of Alupka: though not for the buildings as finally completed. By the end of 1823, Vorontsov had already acquired other properties on the south coast of the Crimea. Early in 1824, he settled on Alupka as the site of his future home, and entered into negotiations with the local Tatar land-owners, through an intermediary, Feodosi Revelioti, commander of a local guard battalion. One of the terms of the deal ultimately agreed upon was that Vorontsov should build a new mosque for the local population, a condition to which he readily assented. The site already enjoyed the benefit of plantings carried out in 1787 for Potemkin by William Gould, including two huge cypress trees.

The Count then recruited the German garden-master Karl Kebach who worked in close collaboration with Nikolai Gartvis, the Director of the nearby Nikita Botanical Gardens, then and still very notable, from which many of his

---

1   *Gentleman's Magazine*, XCIX, 1, 1829, pp. 468–70.
2   *The Modest Genius*, 1977.
3   Information from Mrs Anna Galichenko, of Alupka Palace.

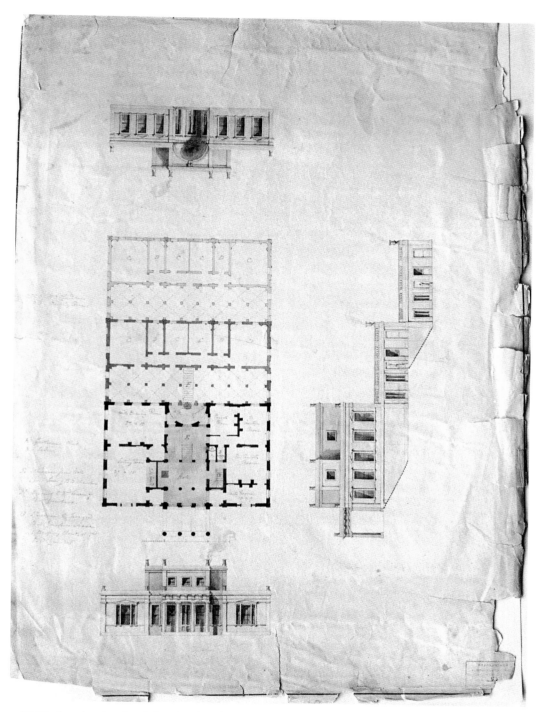

27. Unsigned and undated drawing for plan, entrance façade, seaward façade and side elevation for Alupka Palace, attributed to Thomas Harrison of Chester.

Alupka Archive.

28. Detailed enlargement of previous illustration, showing the original proposal for an arched recess or exedra in the centre of the seaward façade at Alupka, subsequently developed into an Indian or Persian-style *Iwan*.   Alupka Archive.

seeds and seedlings – at first, mostly olive trees and cypresses – came: though other contributions flowed in from all over the world. Note that the planning of the gardens, park and subsidiary buildings seems to have preceded the planning of the palace. Soon after his appointment in 1824, it seems that Philip Elson was instructed to build a temporary dwelling for the Count and his family, later known as 'The Asiatic Pavilion' (still standing, but much mutilated); the new mosque; an orthodox church; and a house for the garden-master. But the foundations of the palace were not laid until March, 1830: "Au mois de mars", wrote the Count, "j'ai fait un cours en Crimée et c'est alors que nous avons posé les premières pierres de notre grande maison à Aloupka".[1]

It is clear from C. R. Cockerell's diary that Harrison was already preparing drawings for Vorontsov by November 1823;[2] it seems likely that these were for Odessa rather than for Alupka; Ockrim describes a surviving drawing in Chester as "rambling and inept". But one very significant drawing does survive in the archive at Alupka:[3] and has been persuasively attributed by the late L. N. Timofeev to Harrison, and dated 1828. "Support of this is the fact that the captions are in English, and the scale is in feet".[4] The handwriting looks like Harrison's; the north portico resembles one by Harrison; there are other classical elements in the design which relate quite closely to some of Harrison's work at Chester.

[1]   Quoted by Shiryaev, in his 'Estate Architecture in the Crimea', in *Krim*, VIII, Simferopol, 1928, p. 86.
[2]   Cockerell, Diary, 9 November 1823, in RIBA Library.
[3]   YN 210 in Box 6, Alupka Archive.
[4]   Timofeev, 'Origins of the Composition of the Vorontsov Palace at Alupka', 1980.

In fact, Harrison's design, though some of the external detailing seems conventional, in its layout is strikingly original and unconventional. In essence, the main body – comprising the formal rooms of the house – is on the ground (yet upper) floor; a small group of rooms, perhaps for the servants, perhaps for the Count and Countess themselves, is placed in a kind of attic above the principal floor; the rest of the house, containing eight bedrooms, and four dressing-rooms, cascades down the steep hillside on two floors below the main level.

Externally, the north, or entrance, front, has a tetrastyle portico, with shallow-pedimented three-light windows, lighting eating-room on the left, ante-room on the right, flanking those of the extravagant central hall. The south, or seawards-facing, front is of six bays, again with shallow pediments, on either side of a great *exedra* or *iwan* looking out over the Black Sea; flanked by Withdrawing Room on the left, Private Room and the Countess's Room on the right; leaving space for the Count's room on the eastward side, a staircase, and privies for the ladies and the gentlemen – very small rooms, but very novel in early nineteenth-century Russia. It is annoying to have no information about the attic storey; though, as it has no windows facing to seaward, it was probably not designed for use by the Count or Countess. But it is exasperating to have the plan of the Eating-room, but no hint as to where were kitchens and service rooms. The Eating-room seems to have three doorways: one from the drawing-room; and two from the hall, by way of small service-rooms or pantries. No sign of a kitchen, or even a passage to a kitchen. Probably, the answer to this conundrum is that (for fear of fire) the kitchen was in a separate building: as was quite common practice in Russia at this time; indeed, as in Blore's eventual design for Alupka; and in Elson's kitchen for the palace at Stilgirka, on the outskirts of Simferopol (see p. 122). But how did the service arrangements work? Is one to suppose that all guests were expected to be always punctual? Or did not late arrivals coincide most inconveniently with the first dishes, since both seem to have had access only through the front door? And, how hot was the food when it eventually arrived on table? At least, Blore was to provide an underground passage from kitchen to dining-room.

It seems that the foundations for the principal block had been laid – or, more exactly, cut into the rocky outcrops of the hillside – before Harrison's death, at the age of eighty-five, on 29 March, 1829; but not those of the lower, bedroom, floors; which were instead turned into the famous lion terraces: whilst the bedroom accommodation was ultimately for the most part provided in the so-called Shuvalov wing, along the rocky outcrop to the east of the main building, or else in a rather more extended upper storey. But, though it was soon abandoned, some highly important elements of this original design were to survive in the palace as finally completed.

29. Edward Blore, architect of Alupka (1787–1879). The only known photograph, taken about 1875 when he was was 88. He had given up practice over 25 years earlier, in 1849.

Photograph: Country Life, 14 December 1945.

VIII: EDWARD BLORE AND COUNT VORONTSOV

It is not known how Blore and Count Vorontsov became acquainted: perhaps simply because both belonged to the same network; perhaps because Vorontsov was a great admirer of Sir Walter Scott and his home at Abbotsford, in whose design Blore had played a modest part; more probably, because of the Count's connection, through his sister the Countess of Pembroke, with the Herbert family of Wilton House: it may be relevant that Blore was working in 1831 on St Mary Magdalene's Hospital, Wilton, for which his drawings are in the Wilton archive.

Edward Blore (1787–1879) started out as a topographical artist, specialising in Gothic buildings: his skill as a draughtsman was to stay with him throughout his long life. In 1816, Sir Walter Scott describes him in a letter to Robert Surtees as "your draughtsman, Mr Blore, a modest and well-bred young man, as well as an excellent artist". The British Museum holds no fewer than 5,092 of his drawings in 48 bound volumes, collected, indexed and mounted by Blore himself.

His active career as an architect lasted only twenty-five years, from 1824 to 1849, when he retired, aged 62, but lived on for another thirty years. During that time, he had designed 21 new churches, enlarged or restored another 21 (including 6 cathedrals), 6 schools, 5 university buildings, 3 royal houses, 2 town halls, 2 almshouses, a hospital, the London Charterhouse, and major works at Lambeth Palace, Windsor Castle, and Buckingham Palace: and his country house work included 34 houses built from scratch or with major alterations and 18 with minor additions or alterations.[1] This prodigious output was, of necessity, to some extent delegated to assistants and clerks of works; but the drawings are almost all Blore's own. He never travelled to the Crimea, nor to Sydney for which he drew plans for the Governor's house in 1835; but he visited work in progress in Ireland at Crom Castle, Ballydrain House, and Castle Upton on eleven occasions between 1830 and 1838;[2] and travelled extensively through England and Scotland from his Welbeck Street base.

"By the 1820s Blore had made the transition from an antiquarian draughtsman to a practising architect ... he soon gained the reputation of being a

[1] Reeves-Smyth, 'An Elizabethan Revival House in Ireland', in *Avenues to the Past*, 2003, pp. 323–4.
[2] *Ibid.*, p. 325.

30. water-colour perspective of the design for Alupka Palace, with colourful Tatars and mountainous landscape, by Edward Blore. This was his vision for the palace, and it turned out pretty much as he envisaged it: even the gushing stream is in the right place, although he never went to the Crimea and never saw his handiwork.

Drawings Collection, Victoria and Albert Museum.

31. The Alupka Palace as actually built, although before the layout of the formal gardens or the installation of the marble lions on the seaward staircase were complete. Gouache of 1842 by Carlo Bossoli. The Indian-style look-out pavilions on the roof, shown also in Blore's original drawings, were for some reason removed before 1850 – much to the benefit of the overall design.

Private collection, reproduced by courtesy of Sayn-Wittgenstein Fine Art, New York.

thoroughly trustworthy architect whose estimates were to be relied upon ... Energetic and reliable, Blore built up an extensive practice both as a country-house architect and as a designer and restorer of churches. The 'Tudor' and 'Elizabethan' styles were his speciality". But, opines Colvin, "A dull competence pervades all his work".[1]

In 1963, Goodhart-Rendel wrote, unjustly in my view, "I doubt if Blore ever did anything original in his life". Mark Girouard likewise takes the view that Blore was a bit of a bore. "In 1833 Edward Blore was scornfully dismissed by the Duchess of Sutherland as 'the *cheap* architect' ... Blore was never flashy; his buildings were gently picturesque and gently Elizabethan – in the good Old English style. He gave them just enough intricacy to suit the taste of the times but not enough to push the bill up unreasonably. His drawings are remarkably attractive, his buildings often remarkably feeble. His planning was competent but, by the 1840s, a little old fashioned".[2] Girouard goes on to suggest that the hard core of Blore's clientèle were Tory gentry: certainly, they were almost all gentry; and certainly, the Herbert family were Tories; but Meller has queried this: "In addition to the Queen herself, Blore could count a Prince, three Dukes, a Marquess, eleven Earls and eighteen other peers amongst his more distinguished clients. Research into the political allegiances of half Blore's clients (chosen at random) reveals twenty Whigs and fifteen Tories".[3]

Blore's work is very much out of fashion at present: in my personal view, he is considerably under-rated. His present low reputation stems in part, I suspect, from his rather unhappy refacing of Buckingham Palace in the 1840s; and partly from the repetitive nature of his detailing. Certainly, at his worst, his work could (like some of his clients?) be dull and boring. But at his best, particularly in the first ten years of his career – as at Goodrich Court; as at Alupka; as in the staircase at Crom – he could be daringly imaginative and original. Only at Goodrich and at Alupka did he indulge himself in the then so-called "Asiatic" style. Externally, Goodrich Court was in a battlemented castellar style, with battered round towers. It was designed to display the remarkable collection of arms and armour assembled by its owner, Samuel Meyrick. Accordingly, "the interior was intended to serve both as a museum and as a private house, so that most rooms were given an individual style to suit the exhibits each housed".[4] They included an Asiatic Ante-Room, with Indian and Moorish armour, and a circular main Asiatic Armoury, containing (*inter alia*) mounted figures of a Mahratta warrior and a Mogul guard, plus a Janissary

[1]   Colvin, *op. cit.*, p. 130.
[2]   Girouard, *The Victorian Country House*, 1979, p. 51.
[3]   Meller, 'Blore's Country Houses', 1974, p. 19.
[4]   Lowe, *Sir Samuel Meyrick & Goodrich Court*, pp. 154, 155.

banner and the armour of a Rajah.[1] No doubt, as Meller has suggested, here lay the germ of Blore's designs for Alupka.[2]

Before Harrison's death, major works on the layout of the roads in the park had been in hand; fortunately, a battalion of sappers commanded by Lieutenant-Colonel Shipilov was available to dynamite the rocky outcrops. By 1828, the Asiatic Pavilion had been completed: it was to provide interim living-quarters for the owners until the new palace was ready for occupation. But in 1831, Vorontsov went off to England to look at parks and gardens there and in the Highlands; it must have been at this time, not long after the death of Harrison, that he fell in with Edward Blore. For an urgent message came back from England to halt all building work immediately, and to send him detailed plans and drawings of the site. Just a year later, in 1832, the first of Blore's copious and meticulous drawings arrived at Alupka. The great majority of his plans and elevations seem to date from the year 1832, though drawings for later extensions and additions run on into the later years of the decade: so late as July, 1837, he was furnishing (per the Countess of Pembroke) his bill of £150 for "A set of plans, Elevations Sections & Working drawings, 58 in number, for a new Library Corridore Lodge Gateway Offices and attached buildings in addition to the House now erecting at Aloupka".[3]

Although Blore himself never travelled to Russia, and so never saw either the site or his palace as built, successive waves of workmen, craftsmen, artificers, and managers arrived in the Crimea in the wake of his drawings. Many were recruited from the Count's various Russian estates: masons, stone-cutters, joiners, cabinet-makers, and wood carvers amongst others. The principal contractors, from 1834 until 1848, were Russian: Gavrila Petrovich Poluektov and his son Ivan. But the supervisory staff were largely English. They were engaged by Vorontsov's London agent, Mr Moberley of the firm of Anderson and Moberley. As the Count wrote to Robert Jackson in February 1833, "I certainly would not have been at the expense of getting over builders from England, if I was not perfectly sure that they would build a thousand times better than we could in the Crimea". Jackson was the 'construction manager', or perhaps rather (in today's idiom), contract manager: known locally as 'Robert Jacoblevich', his descendants are still, I am told, to be found in Moscow.

The first project architect, or clerk of works, was one Francis Heiton, who seems to have worked previously in Blore's London office, and who gave universal satisfaction: unhappily, he died (of a mosquito bite? but not from malaria) in 1833. From the uncommon spelling of his surname, it seems very probable that he was a member of the family of Heiton, minor Scottish landed

---

[1]   Lowe, *op. cit.*, p. 155.
[2]   Meller, *op. cit.*, p. 49.
[3]   Cambridge University Library Ms Add. 3596 (F).

gentry, of Darnick, Roxburghshire, on the outskirts of Melrose. They were thus near neighbours of Sir Walter Scott and among the tenants on their land were John and Thomas Smith of Darnick, the architects, civil engineers and contractors who designed and built Scott's Chiefswood in 1820–21 and contracted for Abbotsford to William Atkinson's designs, incorporating suggestions from Edward Blore, between 1814 and 1824. In the latter year Blore received his first major country house commission, Corehouse, Lanarkshire, for George Cranstoun, Lord Corehouse, a law lord and a member of Scott's circle, probably on Scott's recommendation as he was then unknown as an architect. In the following year, Blore was commissioned to remodel Freeland House, Perthshire for Lord Ruthven, on Scott's recommendation. It was probably work in a similar capacity which enabled Andrew Heiton senior, who was certainly of the Darnick family, to set up a flourishing architectural practice in Perth, in which he was succeeded by his son Andrew Heiton junior. One William Heiton was the very conscientious clerk of works for Blore at Goodrich Court from 1829 until his death in 1833; in recognition of his services, a tower there was named after him (although it only contained the wash-house and laundry). I have been unable to discover the relationship between Andrew, William, and Francis Heiton. It is curious that Andrew Heiton junior, like the client at Goodrich Court, should have been a notable collector of antiquities, particularly armour and weapons. And it seems a strange coincidence that both William and Francis Heiton, two of Blore's most trusted clerks of works, should have died in the same year. On 13 June of that year, the Count wrote to Jackson "I still was very much affected by poor Heiton's death and however useful he was for me, and though that loss is perhaps irreparable for us, my first impression is to regret the man, for I really felt for him both regard and friendship. I have written yesterday to my sister sending her your letter to show to Blore with a copy of the contract we had with Heiton and begging of her, and of Mr Blore, to do everything in their power to engage as quickly as possible a clerk of works as much as possible like Heiton and send him over immediately".[1] The outcome was the appointment, in September 1833, of William Hunt as Heiton's successor; he, too was to give entire satisfaction (see chapter IX, below).

Rather surprisingly, in view of the problems encountered in St Petersburg by Charles Cameron, it does not seem to have been thought necessary to import stone-masons from abroad: they mostly came from Moscow; but it must be said that the quality of the stonework at Alupka, particularly in the very hard local diabase (or greenstone), is of outstanding excellence. The joinery workshop was supervised by an English carpenter, Charles Williams, brought

[1] Transcript in Alupka Library.

out along with Hunt in 1833 at a salary of 3,000 roubles a year: he was to go native, marry a Russian girl, be transported for his own safety by Count Vorontsov to the Moshny estate on the outbreak of the Crimean War, and to leave numerous descendants in Russia. He was assisted by two serfs, Akim Lapshin and Maksim Teslenko, from Moshny; and by a cabinet-maker, Naum Nukhin, from Kostroma. The stucco-work of the blue drawing-room was by Roman Fortunov and four fellow-villagers from Moshny; but the Englishman Edwin Rice was responsible for much of the furniture; and the German Buchner for such of the ironwork as did not come from England. Language problems must, at least at first, have posed severe problems: in January 1833 the Count wrote to Jackson from Odessa, à propos a letter he had received from his neighbour Princess Golitzina, "she mentions something about the interpreters being willing to cause quarrels, *commèrages,* which is exactly the idea I had upon them when I got the last accounts from you and Heiton".

The total number of workers employed on site seemed ever-increasing: in 1833 there were eighty-six; in the ensuing years, around two to three hundred; during the preparations for the visit of Tsar Nicholas I in 1837, around a thousand.[1] Of course, of this enormous number many were working in the park, levelling and rearranging the contours; bringing in the rich black earth of the steppes in baskets; and planting specimen trees from all over the world – mostly acquired, via the Nikita Botanic Gardens, from the firm of Lodge of London – many of them today in their prime.

According to Count Vorontsov's own calculations, the total cost amounted to the staggering figure of nine million roubles in silver: many times more than the cost of a comparable country house in England. Binyon quotes Pushkin as, in 1835, using an exchange rate of 25 paper roubles (*assignats*) to the pound sterling; that would give a cost of £340,000; but the paper rouble was worth only about a quarter of the silver rouble: so that, if the Count really meant silver roubles, we seem to be thinking of the phenomenal figure of £1,360,000 – in early nineteenth-century money, not in today's currency.[2]

It seems certain that the inspiration of this extraordinary complex of buildings owes as much to the client as it does to the architect. Unfortunately, it appears that no correspondence between the two survives. But evidently Vorontsov caused plans of the site, with gradients and contours, together with water-colour drawings of the silhouette of the Ai-Petri mountain, to be sent to London. And it can be inferred that he gave Blore extremely explicit instructions. First, that the silhouette of the palace should reflect that of the mountain range. Second, that the north, or entrance, front of his palace should be of cut stone, in the Tudor Revival style, rather than in Harrison's

[1]   Transcript in Alupka Library.
[2]   Binyon, *Pushkin,* 2002, p. xx.

32. Engraving by Thomas Daniell of the Jummah Musjid mosque in Delhi, published in 1795. This appears to have been the principal inspiration for the design of the seaward front at Alupka: note the detail of the *Iwan*; also the columnar pavilions at the corners of the great courtyard, like those on the roof of Alupka before they were removed. But whether it was Count Vorontsov or Edward Blore who was inspired by this print is not so clear. John Harris remarks, in his *The Architect and the English Country House* of 1985 that Blore built nothing like Goodrich Court either before it or after it, and considers that he was but "the enthusiastic executant of ideas offered by" his client. Maybe the same is true of Alupka?

Illustration from Thomas Daniell's *Oriental Survey*, Part I, 1795.

Neo-Classical style. Third, that the style of the interior should be similar to that employed at Abbotsford. Fourth, that the principal block of the new building should stand on Harrison's foundations, without any significant variations in the plan. Fifth, that Harrison's *exedra* should be completed in the style of a Muslim Iwan as found in the mosques of Persia and Central Asia. And finally, that the whole southern, seaward-facing, façade should be in a style congenial to the predominantly Muslim Tatar inhabitants of the south Crimea.

This might be considered a very tall order, especially as Blore had never previously, save at Goodrich Court, worked in an Oriental style. He had but few precedents to guide him, and had never himself visited the East. There was S. P. Cockerell's Sezincote of 1805; there was John Nash's Brighton Pavilion of 1815; and there was Goodrich Court, Herefordshire, which he had built between 1828 and 1831; but that was almost as much a museum as a country house, kitted out with an Asiatic armoury, whose "gallery extends along three

33. A forerunner of Blore's *Iwan* at Alupka? The Asiatic Armoury at Goodrich Court, Herefordshire, in the Wye valley; designed in 1827 by Edward Blore for the antiquarian Samuel Meyrick. The house, designed to house Meyrick's very notable collection of arms and armour (now for the most part either in the Victoria and Albert Museum or in the Wallace Collection, London), was unhappily demolished in 1949.

The Asiatic Armoury contained, amongst other exhibits, two armoured effigies of warriors on horseback, one a Mahratta, one a member of the Moghul's guard. The great *Iwan* at Alupka appears to owe something to the orientally-arched opening from the Asiatic Ante Room into the main Asiatic Armoury at Goodrich.

Reproduced from J. Skelton, *Engraved Illustrations of the Armour ... at Goodrich Court*, 1830.

sides supported by columns enveloped by weapons and between them and under it, are six and forty figures, ten of which are on horseback".[1] He may, indeed, have derived some inspiration from the Irish architect, James Cavanah Murphy, whose *Arabian Antiquities of Spain* had been published in London in 1813. But his most likely source, particularly for the great central feature of the south front, seems to have been Thomas Daniell's print, published in 1793, of the Jummah Musjid mosque in Delhi.

As to the palace itself: first, the exterior. There were two principal means of access (leaving out of account the path along the shoreline, which must surely have been closed whilst the park was private property): one, the road to the east, leading to the pass between the mountains to Simferopol; the other, the road to Yalta and Sevastopol to the west. It seems as if the main access in earlier days, as now, was from the road to the east; it passes through a battlemented archway, leading to the principal courtyard; but on the left, there is an inconspicuous doorway in the wall, at present blocked, which was the entrance for those seeking business with the Count in his study or library, whose company and muddy boots were not wanted in the front hall – a common enough device in English country houses of the period, but apparently

[1] Skelton, *Antient Armour ... at Goodrich Court*, 1833, *cit.* in Meller, *op. cit.*, p. 48.

71

34. Alupka: the view today, now the trees have grown up, looking uphill from the Black Sea shore, Mount Ai Petri in the background.

Photograph: Paul Barker, Country Life.

35. Alupka: the south-facing seaward front, the central block with the *Iwan*, balconies on cast-iron columns on either side, seen from the staircase of lions, with Mount Ai-Petri in the background.

Photograph: Terence Reeves-Smyth.

36. Alupka, the northern or entrance front, in the English Tudor Revival style (at any rate from the neck downwards).
Photograph: Terence Reeves-Smyth.

unknown in Russia. Past a porter's lodge, this gateway led onto a wide carriage-sweep. To the left, the front of the house, and the principal entrance; to the right, the hillside below the mountain, with all its paths, lawns, plantings, trees, glades, parklands, lakes, cascades, the Great and the Lesser Chaos, and rocky wildernesses.

Ahead, two openings: that to the right, a clock-tower surmounting a two-centred carriage-arch, leading to the stables, coach-houses, kitchens, service quarters, and (formerly) horse-pond; that to the left, giving onto an extra-ordinary narrow, curving, laneway: with only a few arrow-slits, separated by buttresses, opening grimly onto it: giving the impression of a roadway through a medieval fortified town, and leading on to the westward gateway, again battlemented, flanked by two circular towers of uneven height (though Blore had planned that they should be octagonal, Hunt slightly altered their alignment, and made them round). There is a high cast-iron bridge over this alleyway, dramatically providing the only access to the musicians' gallery in the great dining-hall; and a stone basement-tunnel underneath it leading from the kitchens, in the service block, to the pantry beside the dining-room. All of this is very reminiscent of the Welsh and Scottish borders, and much in the romantic style of Sir Walter Scott.

The principal entrance façade is no less Britannic in character. As Andor Gomme remarks, "There is probably no Jacobean house which Alupka closely resembles *in toto*; but all the details come from things that were generic in the early seventeenth century, some a bit earlier. If you want to start with one house, you could do worse than Keele Hall, which he certainly knew, because he worked there before Salvin completely recast the house. The general lines of the Alupka front are not unlike those of the original south front of Keele".[1] To most English visitors it seems little more than another, rather repetitious, early-Victorian stone mansion in the Tudor-Revival style, with label-mouldings above the windows, stone mullions and transoms dividing up their up-to-date plate-glass, a symmetrical arrangement of advancing and receding bays, colonettes at their corners, and a strongly emphasised central doorcase with sculpted heads at the bottom of the dripstones and fancy ironwork lampholders. And, from the neck downwards, they are not mistaken; for this is just such an English-style country-house as Count Vorontsov wanted. But, from the parapet upwards, how very different! The corner towers culminate in Oriental-style cupolas; each colonette rises to a stone finial in the Oriental taste; the tall array of chimney-stacks which crowns the silhouette is astonishing; even the machicolations of the parapet take on an Eastern character. This, and indeed the other remarkable elements in the roofscape, are all best appreciated from the flat lead roof itself: unfortunately, not normally open to the public. There were originally two Oriental pavilions with onion domes on the roof, presumably for surveying the incomparable views all around, but these were taken down during the 1840s or 1850s: it must be said, to the considerable benefit of the composition. It is perhaps a little unfortunate that the Oriental trimmings so characteristic of the south front spill over the roofline to provide a somewhat incongruous element topping the north front: had Blore chosen to employ a pitched roof, this could have been successfully disguised; but that was not his style.

The south front, looking out over the wine-dark sea, is Blore's imaginative triumph: this is a fairy-tale structure worthy of Haroun-al-Rashid and the Arabian Nights. Light and airy, with its oversailing eaves and balconies designed to give shade, it comprises a variegated filigree of glass, stone, and cast-iron. The delicacy of the carved stonework is astonishing; it could only have been secured by the use of the immensely fine yet hard local stone; whose qualities, however,

---

[1]   Andor Gomme, private communication.

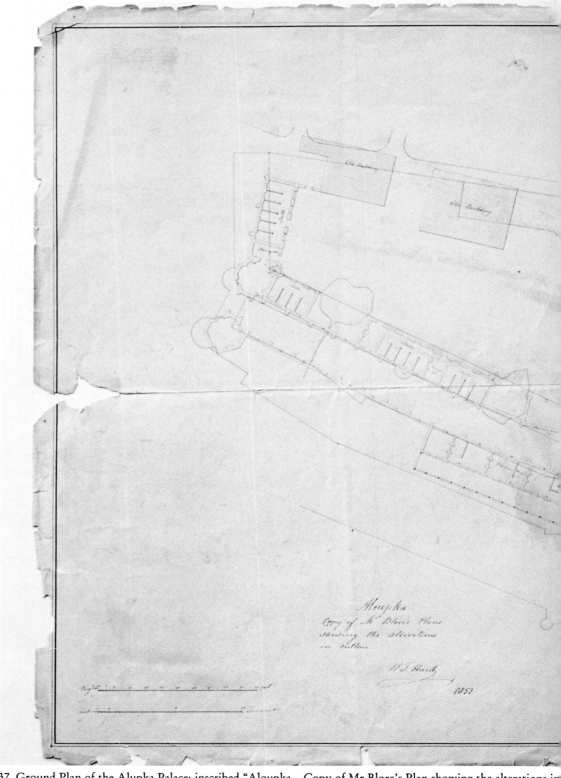

Aloupka
Copy of Mr Blore's Plans
showing the alterations
in outline

W J Hunt

1851

37. Ground Plan of the Alupka Palace: inscribed "Aloupka – Copy of Mr Blore's Plan showing the alterations in
– W J Hunt – 1851". Since this is a copy of Blore's original drawing of about 1832, it shows only the outlin
library block, at the lower right-hand corner, added in the 1840s. Hunt's principal alterations are in the shape and

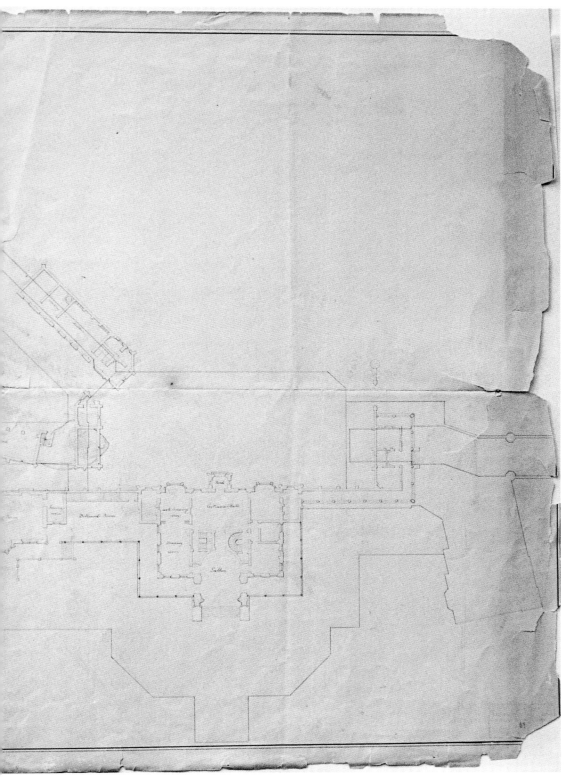

...owers at the western entrance to the Shuvalov passage, and the alignment of the western block of stabling in the courtyard.

...ing YN 795 in the Alupka Archive, photographed by Terence Reeves-Smyth.

cannot have been known to Blore beforehand, although they were greatly appreciated by Hunt. The cast-iron columns that support the balconies, topped by mop-headed capitals of drooping leaves – "slim twisted columns topped with lotus flower capitals"[1] were brought over by ship from England.

The central feature of the south front is, of course, the great two-storey *Iwan*. Originally, it was entirely Indian (or Persian) in conception; but later, Moorish elements derived from the Alhambra were, quite appositely, added. These consisted of three small interior balconies, like swallows' nests, of wood, with cast-iron railings; and six identical Arabic inscriptions, to the effect that 'Allah alone is the victor', derived from the family motto of the Nasrides, first builders of the Alhambra. These changes were made in the 1840s; it has been suggested that the choice of text was a rueful one on the part of Vorontsov, when in 1844 he was appointed Commander-in-Chief of the armies of the Caucasus, engaged on a never-ending struggle with the Muslim tribes living between Russia and Persia, including the peoples of Chechnya and Daghestan. But, despite these changes, the *Iwan* still corresponds closely with Blore's drawings: as does the delicacy of its interior fittings and ornamentation. Its impressive character has been much enhanced by the decision, likewise of the 1840s, to substitute four terraces leading down the steep hillside for one; and in 1848, a total of six Italian marble lions, carved by Giovanni Bonanni, for the original two.

The central block is two bays wide on each side of the *Iwan*, with a tall pointed double window in each bay; the upper storey contained the family's own bedrooms. To the left, now glazed in but originally open, was the Winter Garden: and to the left of that, the tall block containing the great dining-hall, with its magnificent one-and-a-half storey windows and central oriel; then to the left of that again, the billiard room. The levels now change, and a very long, much lower, two-storey range contained guest-rooms, terminating in the towers of the western gateway.

As to the interior: it is of much interest to compare Harrison's original ground-plan;[2] with Blore's original ground-plan;[3] and with Hunt's comparative ground-plan of the house as finally built.[4] Clearly Blore retained Harrison's original foundations for the central block, and the arrangement of the great seaward *Iwan*, which Blore (oddly) annotates as 'Saloon': though it was to perform that function, as a half-outdoor reception-room, on summer evenings, when Rachmaninov and Chaliapin performed here together in 1898. But Harrison had disposed the Count's and Countess's private apartments to the

1   Meller, *op. cit.*, p. 49.
2   YN O 217 in the Alupka Archive.
3   SD 91/2/(1) in the RIBA Drawings Collection, London.
4   YN 795 in the Alupka Archive.

right of the entrance hall, with the withdrawing-room and eating-room to the left: whereas Blore's original scheme placed the masculine apartments for the Count, his valet, dressing-room (?), butler, library, and billiard-room, to the left of the entrance hall, with a great double drawing-room for the Countess to the right. It seems, however, that she was not having that. The drawing-room remained, but the original billiard-room gave way to a boudoir and small private room for her own use, whilst, until the library was built much later, the Count and his secretary were confined to quite modest rooms with no views to seaward.

Some major changes were made to Blore's earliest plan, and some quite substantial later additions, though in outline it remained unaltered. The most material of the alterations were, the glazing-in of the Winter Garden linking the dining-hall with the central block of the house; and the re-siting of the kitchen nearer the dining-hall, with a link through a subterranean passage, five coach-houses being relocated on the far side of the stable-yard instead.

Of the additions, the most significant were the addition of a range of visitors' bedrooms in the Shuvalov wing; the clock-tower over the archway giving access from the stables to the front sweep; and the building of a whole new range on the far side of the, now-enclosed, stable-yard. There was now stabling for nineteen horses, with a horse-pond fed by a mountain stream and flowing through the gardens below the house, and for ten carriages. In 1846, the new library, waiting room, strong-room, and private access courtyard were added,[1] though, unlike the billiard room, these last had been adumbrated in the original ground plan.

All the principal rooms had elaborate geometrical inlaid parquet floors; oak panelling, in some instances carved in linenfold pattern, up to chair-rail level; oak window-shutters, doors, and door-surrounds; and elaborately-carved ceilings. The imposing front entrance hall, with its emphatic wallpaper and full-length portraits, was particularly British in character. The great dining-hall had two intricately-carved mantelpieces of the local diorite, with carved wooden over-mantels, flanking a cool central fountain of blue and white china: above that, a musicians' gallery. According to Anna Galichenko, "the hall was designed as a hall of knighthood, and was probably adorned with trophies and coats of arms".[2] Four large paintings of Roman scenes by Hubert Robert were incorporated into the over-mantels and walls; and enormously tall pointed Norman-style windows, which, together with the draughts drawn in through the chimneys, allowed the cool breezes from the sea to cool the heats of high summer.

---

[1]   8738.6 in the Victoria and Albert Museum Print-Room.
[2]   Galichenko, 1992, *op. cit.*, p. 24.

The drawing room was not panelled, but was ornamented with white-on-bright-blue flowers and tendrils in stucco, covering not only walls but ceiling too; it was originally furnished in the oriental manner, though now in a not inappropriate Empire style. By August 1836, wrote the Count to his wife, "the arabesques in the drawing-room have been half completed: this is really the most beautiful thing in the world".[1] The Countess's boudoir was panelled and furnished in a kind of Russo-Chinese style: "Evidently she liked to rise early and see the sunrise on the sea, since she chose a place with windows looking north-east. Four high gabled windows – which were also doors onto the veranda – when opened wide converted the otherwise minuscule interior into the likeness of a summer-house".[2]

The Count's splendid library was closely modelled on that of Sir Walter Scott at Abbotsford, with medieval-style knops and mouldings in the ceiling; it contained Chippendale-style furniture, and eighteenth-century English globes. The 24,000 books included many French works of an enlightenment or even revolutionary tendency not normally allowed in Russia. The librarian, an Englishman named Alexander Graves, prepared the principal catalogue in French, though English books from the library at Odessa were catalogued by him in English. Above the mantel-piece still hangs a portrait of Vorontsov's friend, the Catholicos of the local Armenian church and educationalist, Nerses V, evidencing the breadth of his interests and sympathies. The billiard room, or Games Room, was tacked on to the Dining-Hall block in 1844; it housed not only billiard-table (quite recently rescued from a local sanatorium) but also card-tables and musical instruments.

Most of the finest pictures in the house, including an oil painting by Hogarth of a short-sighted gentleman (one Mr Tibson, of the Strand) setting fire to his tricorne hat with a candle, purchased by the Count at Christie's in 1832, are in this room.[3] The Winter Garden contains a number of white marble pieces of statuary, including the Count, his father Simon, the Countess, and Catherine the Great; also a bust of William Pitt the younger by Roubiliac; as well as rare figs, palm-trees, araucarias, and plants from many parts of the world.

But the most interesting example of Blore's versatility in planning is to be seen in his treatment of staircases and lavatories intertwined. Very different indeed from the extraordinary, and almost exactly contemporary, Gothick staircase he designed for Colonel John Creighton, third Earl of Erne, at Crom Castle, County Fermanagh, in Northern Ireland. Of this, Hugh Montgomery-Massingberd writes: "the most spectacular feature is the great Staircase Hall, with its double-return 'Imperial' staircase ... This remarkable interior has the

1   Galichenko, *ibid.*
2   Galichenko, *ibid.* p. 140.
3   Lillford, 'Hogarth's The Politician', 1983, p. 100.

38. The library at Alupka: quite closely, and very deliberately, modelled on Sir Walter Scott's library at Abbotsford, with which both the Counts Vorontsov, father and son, were quite well acquainted. At the time of writing the library is not on view to the public, due to problems with its substructure. The last part of the palace to be completed: Blore's drawings for this were dated 1843.

Photograph: Terence Reeves-Smyth.

39. Crom Castle, by Blore, of exactly the same date as Alupka; the great feudal feast given by Colonel Creighton to celebrate the completion of his new house, in August 1838. All the tenantry are wearing identical dove-grey tail-coats, and top hats, perhaps presented to them for the occasion. Note too that all those at table appear to be males. This anonymous water-colour well exemplifies the medievalising tastes of many of Blore's clients.

Photograph by Terence Reeves-Smyth; original in Crom Castle.

feel of a cathedral, a feeling enhanced by the late Perpendicular arcade, crisply detailed ... which frames the staircase".[1] Rowan calls it "a dramatic staircase entrance rising in a straight flight to the central hall ... certainly the grandest moment at Crom, with a double return staircase – rather like Smirke's Lowther – rising behind a late Perp arcade crisply detailed in timber and plaster. Above is a galleried upper hall, lit by an octagonal 'Elizabethan' roof-lantern".[2]

In total contrast, the twin staircases at Alupka are humble and inconspicuous creatures, tucked away behind closed doors on either side of the narrow passage giving access from the hall to the great central saloon: one circular, one rectangular, presumably one for the family, one for the servants, but it is hard to say now which is which. Nonetheless, Blore's drawings for

[1]   Massingberd & Sykes, *Great Houses of Ireland*, 1999, pp. 60, 61.
[2]   Rowan, *North West Ulster*, 1999, pp. 222–3.

40 (previous page). Blore's extravagantly splendid staircase at Crom Castle, County Fermanagh: exactly contemporary with his drawings for Alupka, but in complete contrast to his hole-and-corner treatment of the staircases there.

Photograph: Christopher Simon Sykes.

41 (left). The actual stair case at Alupka: dark, cramped, and could not be more of a contrast to Blore's contemporary staircase at Crom.

Photograph: Terence Reeves-Smyth.

Crom[1] have a number of features in common with his drawings for Alupka; he must have been working on both more or less simultaneously. In particular, details for swirling ceiling bosses and such-like ornaments are almost identical; and especially similar, the beautifully-drawn detailed drawings for the complex sliding and folding doors dividing the drawing-rooms in two, and for the window-shutters in the bays, for both houses.[2]

However, perhaps Blore's most interesting and original arrangement was in the disposition of the lavatories. He was always keen to provide adequate and up-to-date facilities: at Crom he provided six lavatories, including one for the maid-servants. As Anna Galichenko has remarked, "A big novelty for estate building in Russia was the installation in the palace of sewage disposal and hot water".[3] Before this, a privy, in Russia as in England and Ireland, normally consisted of a circular hole cut out of two planks, housed in a garden shed above

[1] D 1939/2/23 in Public Record Office of Northern Ireland, Belfast.
[2] YN 792 in the Alupka Archive.
[3] Galichenko, 1992, *op. cit.*, p. 21.

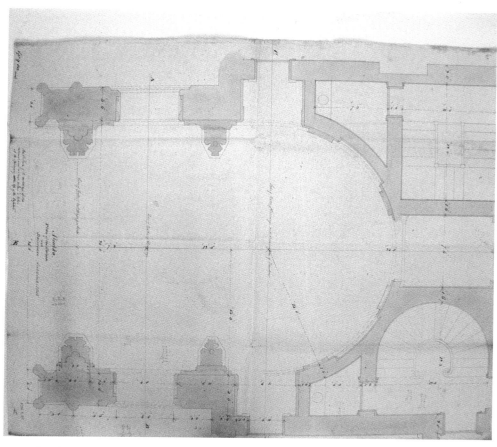

42. Plan, by Blore, of the rear section of the *Iwan*, showing how neatly the two water closets (amongst the first, if not *the* first, in a Russian palace) have been fitted into corners between the curved back wall and the concealed twin staircases.

Victoria and Albert Museum, Prints and Drawings Collection, 8735 A 45, dated September 29th, 1832. Photograph by Terence Reeves-Smyth.

a bucket, a cess-pit, or (if one was lucky) a stream. I have myself, in the late 1940s, before sewers and mains water were general in country districts, made use of such facilities both in rural Ireland and rural France; I am sure they still survive in other, less privileged, parts of the world. But Blore rose above this: on 11th May, 1833, the Count wrote "William Moberley has shipped on a Colombian packet from Constantinople and Odessa the 24 cast iron pillars for the house, 6 dozen shovels by order of Mr Blore ... one box containing iron blocks etc., one box tools, saws, etc., 12 water closets with a quantity of lead pipe ...".[1] Where they were all distributed is something of a mystery; on Blore's original plan, the principal two are shown neatly fitted into the spaces left over

[1]   Letter from Odessa, 11 May 1833, transcript in the Alupka Archive.

87

between the stairs and the semi-circular back walls of the Saloon; and one other, to serve all the guest-rooms (no *en-suite* facilities then). Unfortunately, none of the original fittings at Alupka seems to have survived: but it is likely that they were constructed to the designs of Joseph Bramah, whose patent had been taken out in 1778, but whose closets were to remain the accepted pattern in Britain until about 1890.[1]

By June 1834, work was well under way. The Maréchal Marmont arrived for a four-day visit on the 15th, and found work well in train, though he had to stay in the Asiatic House. "La maison occupé aujourd'hui n'est que provisoire; une autre est commencée, sur les plus vastes dimensions. Cette superbe demeure rappellera les plus beaux châteaux d'Angleterre, pour lesquels le style gothique est adopté. Tout y est conçu sur une vaste échelle. Ce sera le digne séjour du créateur de la Crimée, et le chef-lieu convenable d'une grande fortune ..."[2]

43 (opposite). The great dining hall, Alupka, showing the elaborate timber ceiling and parquet floor; two of the four paintings by Hubert Robert; one of the two elaborately-carved fireplaces; and the balcony of the musicians' gallery; together with the comparatively modest dining-table and chairs at present on display.

Photograph: Paul Barker, Country Life.

[1]   Wright, *Clean and Decent*, 2000, p. 107.
[2]   Raguse, Duc de, *Voyage*, 1837, p. 319.

44. The Alupka dining-hall, probably late 1870s or 1880s. The original dining-table, with chairs for fifty, has gone, probably removed to Italy by Prince Simon's widow after his death in 1882; but what has happened since then to the splendid candelabra? Note too the painted fillets around the cornice: when inserted and when removed?

Photograph: Orlov of Yalta, the first professional photographer in the Crimea; author's collection.

45 (opposite). The salon, music-room or so-called Seraskier Room, Alupka: at first, furnished throughout in the Ottoman style; alas, no photographs or engravings of the room as it originally appeared seem to have survived, and the original furnishings have now all gone, to be replaced (not inappropriately) by furniture, and a piano, in French Empire style. Note the remarkable blue-and-white stucco decoration.

Photograph: Paul Barker, Country Life.

46 (above). The Winter Garden as it is today, housing a mixture of exotic greenery and sculpture, linking the principal room the dining-hall. Originally, it was open but it was not long before it was glazed-in.

Photograph: Paul Barker, Country Life.

47 (opposite page). 'Aloupka, Intérieure des galeries du Jardin d'Hiver'; photograph of about 1885. interesting to compare this with the previous illustration: note the total absence of sculpture numerous chairs, and the globes of gasoliers.

Photograph by Orlov of Yalta; author's collection.

48 (above). The Billiard (or Games) Room at Alupka. This room seems to have been an after-thought, added to Blore's orig
plan in the 1840s, presumably by Hunt. The billiard table itself was rescued from a nearby sanatorium. This room contains m
of the best paintings in the house, including the only oil painting by William Hogarth (of a short-sighted politician accident
setting his hat on fire) in Russia.

Photograph: Terence Reeves-Smyth.

49 (opposite page). The great *Iwan* or *Exedra* of Alupka Palace, seen from the upper terrace, with
first pair of Bonanni's marble lions in front. Although often described as Moorish, and even in Co
Vorontsov's day called the 'Alhambra', this is clearly Moghul in conception. To Blore's work
Count later, in the 1840s, and by no means inappropriately, added three balconies and two Ar
inscriptions derived from the Alhambra.

Photograph: Terence Reeves-Smyth.

50. The view from the central balcony of the *Iwan*. The Black Sea, in which dolphins are sometimes to be seen tumbling and playing, lies far below; the lion staircase and the terraced gardens with their carefully-placed yew trees lead the eye down to the sea.
   Photograph: Terence Reeves-Smyth.

51 (opposite, above). Alupka: the front gravel with, to the left, the entrance to the Shuvalov passage; to the right, the archway giving access to the kitchens, service courtyard, stables and coach-houses; and to the right of that, the clock tower, set at an angle to the front courtyard. The Victorian creepers and climbers here shown have now been cut down.
   Photograph by Orlov of Yalta, probably *c*. 1885; author's collection.

52 (opposite, below). The Shuvalov passage, with Victorian creepers and climbers (now removed), facing the western gateway.
   Photograph by Orlov of Yalta, probably *c*. 1885; author's collection.

53. The tall, dark and narrow Shuvalov Passage, with its almost total absence of openings, was intended to convey the feeling of an alley-way in a medieval town, and succeeded admirably. The family and public rooms to the south of the Passage all faced the sea. The kitchen and servants' quarters, to the north, all opened onto the courtyard, not onto the Passage. Because of fire risks, the kitchen was in the northern block, and the food reached the dining room through an underground tunnel to the butler's pantry adjoining the dining-hall; whilst above ground the musicians reached their gallery in the hall by means of the cast-iron foot-bridge from the servants' quarters.

Photograph: Terence Reeves-Smyth.

54. The western gateway, flanked by the two round towers substituted by Hunt for Blore's original octagonal ones. The barred gate gives access to the Shuvalov Passage; to the left, hidden by bushes, is the gateway opening onto the stables courtyard.

Photograph: Terence Reeves-Smyth.

55 (above, left). Detail of the corner of the central block and the winter garden at Alupka. The slim cast-iron columns were certainly imported from England; it seems likely that the elegant cast-iron railings on the ground floor and balcony were likewise imported, rather than cast locally.

56 (above, right). Detail of stonework at roof level. The delicate filigree of stone echoes that of the ironwork below, and the arrises are all as sharp and clear as the day they were carved, notwithstanding their exposure to the winter gales of the Black Sea for 150 years.

57 (below, right). Another example of elegantly-detailed stone carving: a corner finial surmounting two of the extraordinarily subtly-shaped machicolations designed by Blore. The village of Alupka and the craggy peaks of Ai-Petri appear in the background, above the boskage of the park.

Three photographs: Terence Reeves-Smyth.

58 (above, left). One of Edward Blore's meticulously detailed drawings for Alupka.
  Victoria and Albert Museum, prints and Drawings Collection, No. 8735.20.
59 (above, right). Alupka chimney as built.
60 (below). A stack of seven chimneys.

Three Photographs: Terence Reeves-Smyth.

61 (above). Roofscape, mountainscape, pinnaclescape and chimneyscape: Blore's romantic roofline at Alupka, seen from the roof itself.

62 (below). The central feature of the Lower Park was the great marble staircase flanked by six splendid life-size white marble lions by Bonanni of Bologna, transported here in the 1840s with unimaginable labour; to one of which Winston Churchill took a great fancy.

Photographs by Terence Reeves-Smyth.

63 (above). The Lower Park occupies the steep slope between the Alupka Palace and the shoreline of the Black Sea. It is laid out in marble staircases, terraces and pathways leading down to the little Grecian tea-house by the shore.

64 (below). The Upper Park was deliberately laid out on the model of an English country house park: Count Mikhail Vorontsov had travelled widely in England in the 1830s seeking ideas.

Photographs by Terence Reeves-Smyth.

65 (above). Amongst the features of the Upper Park are the Greater and the Lesser Chaos. These are man-made, very Romantic and Byronic, piles of great boulders, almost surreal in character. This picture shows the Great Chaos from below. It is regrettable that an intrusive modern bungalow should have been allowed to be built on the hillside above it. Photograph by Terence Reeves-Smyth.

66 (below). The Upper Pond, Alupka, in a light snowfall in early 2004.
Photograph by Vladimir Dmitrenko.

67. 'Aloupka, Vue de l'Alhambra': photograph by Orlov of Yalta of about 1885. The *Iwan* was often, erroneously, referred to in the late-19th century as 'the Alhambra', despite the fact that only its later ornaments are Moorish; its architectural character is fundamentally Moghul. A more intriguing question, however, is how was this photograph taken? It could today, on a notably difficult site, only be taken from the air. Did the photographer clamber up some tall tree, now chopped down, which appears on no old print or photograph? Or, more likely, did he employ a balloon?

Photograph: Orlov of Yalta, *c.* 1885, author's collection.

68. The north front of the Alupka Palace, with flag flying: drawing of 1851 by W. J. Hunt, who was almost as accomplished a draughtsman as his master, Edward Blore.

Drawing in Alupka Archive, photographed by Terence Reeves-Smyth.

69. The south, or seaward-facing, front of the Alupka Palace: drawing of 1851 by W. J. Hunt.

Drawing in Alupka Archive, photographed by Terence Reeves-Smyth.

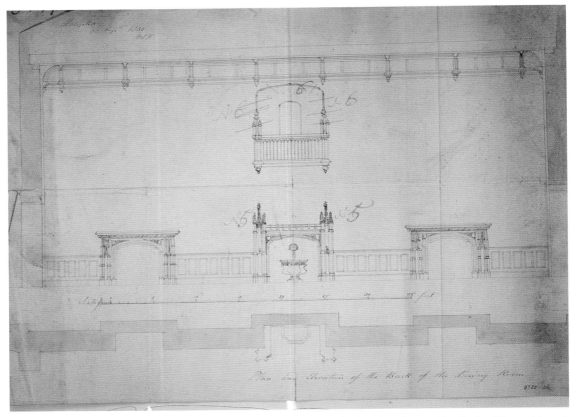

70. 'Plan and Elevation of the back of the Dining Room' at Alupka; drawing, evidently by Hunt although amongst Blore's papers, so probably dating from Hunt's apprenticeship to Blore. The drawing shows the rear wall of the dining room very much as built: two fireplaces, between them an alcove with a fountain for hot weather; above that, the musician's gallery, reached by a cast-iron footbridge over the Shuvalov Passage from the kitchen block.

Victoria and Albert Museum, Prints and Drawings Collection, 8735.26. Photographed by T. Reeves-Smyth.

"macademised roadway" for forty miles; not only did he instruct the local workmen in many techniques new to them, such as plumbing; not only did he achieve a remarkably high standard of wood-working in all the joinery, parquet, and cabinet-making; as Anna Galichenko remarks "Hunt showed genuine flair in dealing with building materials, displaying to advantage the qualities of diabase, its colour and composition".[1] In 1838, the Countess wrote to her husband: "Hunt dit lui-même, que vu la beauté de la pierre, il n'y a vu d'aussi beau en Angleterre".[2]

Indeed, particularly in the later years, when the Count was much away in the Caucasus, Hunt seems to have executed a number of completely new works,

[1]   Galichenko, *op. cit.*, 1992, p. 20.
[2]   Transcription by E. H. Timoleev in Alupka Archive.

71. The so-called 'Bakhchisaray Courtyard' at Alupka, by Hunt, who successfully (and ingeniously) designed and constructed the copy of the Fountain of Tears in the centre of the court. Note the delicacy of the cast-iron columns supporting the wistaria-clad pergola.   Photographed by Terence Reeves-Smyth.

not envisaged by Blore, including the so-called Bakhchisaray courtyard, with its copy of the Fountain of Tears, designed in 1851, in memory of Pushkin's well-known poem, and perhaps of the Countess's earlier fling with him in Odessa: and the Georgian courtyard below; the installation of a pair of Florentine fountains, some marble flower-pots shaped like Roman sarcophagi, eight metal statues imported from Trieste, and many minor stonework features, fountains, and monuments in the park and gardens. He had of course already been responsible for the completion of the Shuvalov range (named for Vorontsov's daughter, Sofiya, who married Count Shuvalov in 1844, and thereafter used these rooms for the holiday accommodation of their family), after the insertion of the billiard room; for the gateway with its round towers at the end of the Shuvalov passage; and for the completion of the outbuildings enclosing the kitchen courtyard: none of which had figured in Blore's original plan. And, in the early 1840s, Hunt and Kebach were paid the enormous sum of 24,473 roubles 55 kopecks towards the cost of remodelling the terraces to the seaward

72. Alupka Palace and subsidiary buildings, as finally completed: lithograph of 1855 by W. Timm. Centre: the palace itself, designed by Blore, executed by Hunt. Note that the two pavilions on the roof, shown in earlier pictures, have by now disappeared. Extreme left: the so-called Asiatic Pavilion, probably by Elson, in which the Vorontsov family lived while the principal mansion-house was being built. Upper left: the Mosque built for Count Vorontsov by Elson, for the use of the local Tatar villagers. The school-house, and the house of Karl Kebach, the German head gardener, are off-picture to the left. The presumably-temporary tent-like building, lower-left, is a mystery. At the centre, below, is the Grecian tea-house built by Elson behind St George's little harbour, through which most of the building materials were carried. Looming up at the rear: the crags of Mount Ai-Petri.

Print in the Alupka Archive: photograph by Vladimir Dmitrenko.

side of the Iwan: "The hill in front of the Big House at Alupka has been removed and the site re-planned. It has become extremely beautiful".[1] In the course of this work, it was necessary to provide strong supporting foundations to minimise the risk of damage from landslides, common all along this coast. Fortunately soldiery were on hand to carry out much of the work; when they left in November 1841, after a year's earth moving, Vorontsov was put to the expense of hiring twenty steppe Tatars to finish the job. It seems that Hunt and Kebach worked in close collaboration to complete both park and gardens; with signal success, and to the entire satisfaction of their employers. Hunt's honourable retirement, and generous pension, have already been noted. It would seem that they had been well-deserved.

73. Alupka, north-facing front and buildings to the east photographed in the slight snowfall of early 2004.   Photograph by Vladimir Dmitrenko.

[1]   Galichenko, *op. cit.*, 1992, p. 26.

X: PHILIP ELSON AND COUNT VORONTSOV

Count Michael Vorontsov was officially appointed Governor-General of New Russia in May 1823; and arrived in Odessa to take up his duties at the end of June. He was then aged thirty-eight. Philip Elson was appointed Chief Architect for the South Coast of New Russia in 1824, aged thirty-four. Although Elson was never invited to participate in any way in the design of Alupka Palace itself, it is clear that he quickly established an excellent rapport with his new Chief, who no doubt welcomed the appointment of so cosmopolitan a near-contemporary to so sensitive a post. When asked to provide a report on his merits, the Count replied: "as regards the taste, diligence and honesty of this artist, I have had occasion to put them to the test".[1]

He is said to have been the author of "several post-houses, guard-huts and fountains; several buildings on the Emperor's estate at Oreanda; churches at Massandra and Koreiz; and a mosque at Alupka ... and he also built a number of private houses". Unhappily few of these have survived, fewer still unmutilated; and the documents that have survived are extremely sparse. Most of the remaining drawings attributed to him are unsigned; written evidence regarding his authorship of buildings is but seldom forthcoming. But his style is, on the whole, individual and extremely consistent.

"Having thoroughly studied the architecture of the palace of Bakhchisaray and the character of local Tatar buildings which had been preserved, Elson in his projects uses such local elements as the large abutments of cornices covered with subtle wood carving; overhanging glazed balconies and trellised galleries; broad terraces on elegant columns or pillars; pointed windows; ornaments on the roof in the shape of urns; chimneys resembling minarets, and painted ceilings in the 'Asiatic' manner". In his anxiety to cause his designs to fit into their historical environment, Elson was much before his time. But he was eminently capable, when he thought it appropriate, of adopting the strictly Classical, the Gothic, or the Neo-Classical styles.

These buildings gave quite a new character to the southern shores of the Crimea. "After climbing hills of average height, you begin to catch sight along the road of dachas with houses built in the most ingenious way. You see

---

[1] Palchikova, 'F. F. Elson', 1997, p. 186. All the quotations in this chapter are, unless otherwise stated, from this generally authoritative and reliable source: although I have preferred the date on Elson's tombstone to that of 1795, cited by her.

alternately now a small house in the Asiatic taste whose windows are concealed by shutters and whose chimneys are like minarets, now a beautiful Gothic castle, now a cosy little dacha, like an English cottage, completely drowned in a sea of flowers and greenery, and now a light wooden building with extensive galleries".[1] Although this was written in 1837, and published in 1853; and although Stalin's enormous neo-classical sanatoria and holiday homes, along with modern houses and blocks of flats, have greatly changed the once wild and beautiful landscape, one can still see something of what the author meant.

74. The Asiatic Pavilion, used as a temporary home to Count Vorontsov and his family while Alupka was a-building; and fountain attributed to Elson (and, if so, one of his first buildings for the Count, of 1825).
  Print by J. Maurer, 1829.

75 (opposite). The central atrium and fountain of the Grecian tea-house by the sea-shore at Alupka, lithograph of 1834 by Aniskerich, from a drawing by N. Chernetsov.
  Both illustrations from Alupka Archive.

It seems likely that Elson's first work in the Crimea was the so-called 'Asiatic Pavilion' at Alupka, built in 1825 to provide the Count and Countess with a pied-à-terre for their occupation on visits to supervise progress on the palace and the park, although there is no documentary evidence that he designed it.[2] It has, alas, though still standing, been so altered as to be now quite unrecognisable: its original appearance, with verandas not unlike those at the palace itself, is well shown in two lithographs of 1830 by one Wolff.[3] It was

[1]   Demidov, *Journey to South Russia ... in 1837*, 1853, p. 286.
[2]   Both Shiryaev and Palchikova attribute this building to Elson, but Galina Filatova thinks that he would have been too busy at Bakhchisaray and on other official duties, and attributes it to Harrison. On stylistic grounds I doubt this.
[3]   Wolff, lithographs of 1830, reproduced by Galichenko, *op. cit.*, 1992, pp. 18, 19.

vividly described by the ex-Maréchal de Marmont in the course of his stay in June 1834: "Quatre jours s'écoulèrent, pour moi remplis d'agrément, dans l'intimité de cette adorable famille. Le bâtiment provisoire que nous occupions est entouré, des quatre côtés, de vastes et spacieux balcons. C'est là que nous passions nos soirées ... Le jardin, déjà fait en partie, sera délicieux ... Avant de quitter Aloupka, je plantais dans le jardin un tulipier, auquel madame Woronzow voulut bien donner mon nom..."[1] – the tulip-tree is still there.

One of the lithographs shows also the mosque, built just up the hill on the

edge of the village of Alupka: "its minaret and onion dome stood out against a background of low, flat-roofed buildings. The character of the mosque's architecture accorded with that of Muslim religious buildings. The architect built in the traditional forms evolved in the East, without adding anything new". This was, no doubt, in accordance with the express instructions of his client, the Count, who never passed over an opportunity of conciliating the local populations of the Crimea and the Caucasus.

Elson's third building at Alupka appears to have been the seaside Grecian tea-house or pavilion just above the curving pier of the little harbour, known as Port Georges, to which small ships brought building materials from Odessa or Sevastopol. This charming little building, with its fluted Doric columns and central atrium, still stands; but, sadly, its windows have had to be boarded up

[1]   Raguse, Duc de, *Voyage*, 1837, pp. 317–20.

76. The Black Sea, glimpsed between the fluted columns of Elson's Grecian tea-house, just above the little harbour of Port St Georges.

Photograph: Terence Reeves-Smyth.

77 (opposite). Elson's Grecian tea-house today, on the shoreline at Alupka. Unhappily, its windows have had to be boarded up as a result of vandalism. Port St Georges is a very popular swimming-place in summer. It attracts considerable crowds of swimmers, for the coastal path (very rightly) is open to all; but the charming little building cannot, therefore, be allowed to remain unprotected.

Photograph: Terence Reeves-Smyth.

because of vandalism – there is open access to the seashore, and crowds come here to swim in the summer. Galichenko describes it as "a tea-house with the shape of a strict Doric propylaea was supposed, in terms of architectural order, to resonate with the Alupka church (not preserved) which was being erected on the western hill".[1] The tea-house seems to have been nearing completion in 1835. The church, designed by Elson in 1833 but completed (by Hunt) only in 1840, was a much more ambitious affair. "The architect tried to reproduce and repeat almost unchanged the famous temple of Theseus at Paestum ... It was built, exactly as at Paestum, in the shape of a Greek periptery with six Doric columns on the end and nine on the longitudinal sides"[2] ... "It stood out beautifully against the background of the greenery of the lower park and the seascape" ... but "the chancel in the temple is treated not at all in the tradition of antiquity. Along the whole wall a large window was made in the shape of a

[1]   Galichenko, *op. cit.*, p. 23.
[2]   There is a puzzle here: my archaeologist friends say that they know of no temple at Paestum dedicated to Theseus; nor do the plans of the Theseion in Athens correspond to this description. Perhaps the two temples at Paestum have been conflated into one?

cross, which created a particular kind of lighting and intensified the religious mood of the parishioners" (Palchikova).

Another Grecian church by Elson (oddly named 'the Church of the Decapitation of John the Baptist')[1] was built at Massandra between 1829 and 1833. Long since demolished, its appearance is known only from a couple of representations; but it seems to have been delightful. "The church's severe forms and its Doric portico with successfully realised proportions harmonises well with the age-old trees which surrounded it ... All travellers in the Crimea were delighted with this church. Marshall Marmont called it 'entrancing', while Vsevolozhsky wrote 'One should note, at the most elevated point of the highway, a recently completed, beautiful church in Doric style. From beneath its foundations a spring of pure fresh water gushes out, while the church portico is surrounded by walnut trees'" (Palchikova).

The extent of Elson's involvement in the principal house at Massandra is unknown; this seems originally to have been a neo-classical house built in 1829 at the centre of its extensive park (laid out by Karl Kebach) and vineyards. Unfortunately, in 1879 the old mansion-house was severely damaged in a storm.

[1]   Kalinin and Zemlyanichenko, *Romanoff i Krym*, 2002, p. 40.

78 (above). Philip Elson's little church ("Of the Decapitation of John the Baptist") at Massandra, built between 1829 and 1833, now demolished.

Engraving after Bossoli, from the Alupka Archive.

79 (right). Vineyard manager's house, at Massandra, built by Philip Elson in 1831, likewise now gone.

Print in Massandra Archive, photographed by Terence Reeves-Smyth.

MAISON D'INTENDANT À MASSANDRA

80. The main block of the classical house of Stilgirka, on the outskirts of Simferopol. The name of its architect is not known but an attribution to Elson would seem quite plausible, especially in view of the fact that he is known to have designed the separate kitchen block at Stilgirka, athough in quite a different style.
    Photograph: Terence Reeves-Smyth.

In the following year, work started on the present disappointing yellow-brick château designed by the French architect Buchar, who died before it was completed; it was eventually completed as late as 1897 by the German architect Mesmacher for Tsar Alexander III, and subsequently taken over by Joseph Stalin as one of his private dachas; now open to the public, and used as a centre of the Crimean wine trade. It is worth visiting Stalin's lavish private bathroom of the 1930s: a marked contrast from the simpler sanitation of Stilgirka.

The degree of Elson's involvement in the neo-classical stucco house at Stilgirka, standing in a fine park on the outskirts of Simferopol is also uncertain. All that is known with certainty is that he designed the 'Asiatic' free-standing kitchen block.[1] The house itself was built soon after 1826, when Prince Naryshkin, a distant relative of Count Vorontsov and his deputy as Governor of the Crimea, bought the estate from the distinguished scientist, Academician Pallas. It was bought, in turn, by Vorontsov from Naryshkin's widow in 1833.

---

[1]   Naryshkin papers in State Archive, Moscow.

81 (opposite). Detail of the colonnade and railings at the front of Stilgirka. Note the stylistic resemblance to the Grecian tea-house at Alupka, known to have been designed by Elson.

82 & 83. Two views of the kitchen block at Stilgirka, by Elson.   Photographs by Terence Reeves-Smyth.

It has some fine rooms, though it has been considerably altered and added to. Now home to an archaeological institute, it is intended to become an archaeological museum. There are some good painted ceilings of the mid-nineteenth century; an imposing Grecian hall with well restored murals of scenes from Scythian history; a fine library; and a spiral staircase rising from basement to attics. Its sanitary arrangements would not have commended themselves to Edward Blore: they consist of a hole in the basement floor, with two 'footprints', so that the hole may be addressed either from the front or the rear; but no seat of any kind. Both Tsar Nicholas I, and Alexander II, stayed at Stilgirka; it is to be hoped that they appreciated the plumbing.

As to the kitchen, "the oriental character of this small, square, tiled edifice is intensified by decorative turrets at the corners of the roof and by a chimney resembling a minaret" (Palchikova). There are still many Moorish details in its unrestored interior, and much wooden fretwork painted bright yellow. It was originally one great room, but was divided up in 1913 by internal partitions. It is not presently in good order, but is by no means beyond restoration.

Elson also designed for Count L. S. Potocki – a Pole serving in the Russian Diplomatic Corps – the original house at Livadia, which "resembled a small museum of antiquities; the park was adorned with genuine, beautifully preserved, marble sculptures and a sarcophagus from the early Christian period, covered all over with bas-reliefs, while in the house ... there was preserved in one of the studies a collection of antiquities from Pompeii":[1] unhappily destroyed in the late nineteenth century to make way for the distressingly overblown Imperial Palace on the same site.

One of the last groups in the Crimea to be attributed to Elson comprises the mansion and subsidiary buildings at Oreanda, completed in 1831, first built for the vine-grower Feltmann; then acquired by Count Vitt; later to become a royal property. "In all probability, the whole of Vitt's estate at Oreanda was designed by Elson. The entrance into the property is designed in the form of a high gateway, with a lancet arch, enclosed by square pylons with pointed terminals. In its form the gateway is closer to Gothic edifices ... the palace museum of Alupka holds a drawing by Elson, signed by him in 1832, with a plan for an enclosure executed in Gothic style ... in his projects for the Crimea Elson had resort to the use of elements of both oriental and Gothic architecture" (Palchikova).

Other houses: for A. V. Asher, near Ayu-Dagh; Artek, for D. E. Bashmakov at Mshatka; and L. A. Perovsky's house at Mellas; have been tentatively attributed, on stylistic not documentary grounds, to Elson.

---

[1] Kalinin and Zemlyanichenko, *op. cit.*, p. 198.

84. Unsigned and undated drawing, attributed to Philip Elson and inscribed 'Maison pour M. le prince Galizine à Caspra | Face de derrière | Face'.   Drawing in the Alupka Archive photographed by Terence Reeves-Smyth.

The last building in the Crimea which can be attributed with some confidence to Elson is the country house at Gaspra, built between 1831 and 1837, for which unsigned drawings survive in the Alupka archive; built for Prince A. N. Golitsyn (or Galitzin: either way, the name simply means 'Galician'). It is perhaps more interesting for its literary associations than for its architectural merits: Tolstoy, in old age, spent some time here in the winter of 1901–2, and there still hangs in the house an early photograph of him being visited here by Tchekov and Maxim Gorky. Subsequently, the house belonged to the wealthy countess Panina, who offered hospitality here to the Nabokov family in the dark days of 1919; it is described (imaginatively transported to the USA) in his novel *Pnin*; and remembered in his autobiography, *Speak, Memory*; and here, too, Nabokov wrote his poem 'Crim'.

Gaspra is a peculiar house: perhaps the conception of an English country house of a Russian architect, of English descent, who had only heard about, but never seen Britain. It is a kind of compromise between classical and Gothic. The composition, and especially the ground plan, is unusual: a five-bay two-storey castellated central block (the two centre bays advancing, the side bays set back),

85. An early-twentieth-century photograph of Gaspra, as completed by Hunt to Elson's design, between 1831 and 1837: the seaward façade, or 'face de derrière'. Note the curiously Alupka-like pavilion to the left.

Photograph hanging in the hall at Gaspra, copied by Terence Reeves-Smyth.

all with pointed pseudo-Gothic windows, are flanked by two much taller slim octagonal castellated towers, containing spiral staircases; there is neither central entrance, nor central stairway; the main section is fronted in stone, the rest in stucco. Inside, there is a fine central hall with Gothic detailing, quatrefoil motifs and nicely-carved doors: to the rear, a living-room with a complex black steel Gothic mantelpiece; then a large, original, cast-iron conservatory with Gothic glazing; above it, a larger and grander conservatory, both looking south to the sea, of which they must have enjoyed fine views until the woodland greenery (many cypress trees) was allowed to grow too high all around on the steep hillside. Today used, not entirely inappropriately, as a children's holiday home, it is largely embowered in the ivy which grows so luxuriantly in the Crimea. (More the pity, that it is not used to obliterate the many modern excrescences which disfigure the countryside: not least the vista-blockers outside the park at Alupka.)

In 1834, having completed his principal task in the restoration of Bakhchisaray, Elson petitioned to be allowed to retire from his post, and to return to St Petersburg. His petition was granted; his assistant, Karl Ivanovich

126

86. The north-facing, landward, front at Gaspra, by Elson. Note that there is no central entrance doorway on this front, but a pointed doorway in each of the corner towers.   Photograph by Terence Reeves-Smyth.

87. Count Tolstoy, emerging from the doorway in the south-facing seaward façade, about to climb into his two-horse chaise, during the winter of 1901–1902, aged 73. Note the pseudo-Gothic detailing of the windows and door-surround.

Photograph hanging in the hall at Gaspra, copied by Terence Reeves-Smyth.

88. The bust of Philip Elson ('Philippe d'Elson') surmounting his tomb in the Père Lachaise Cemetery, Paris, where he died in 1867, aged 83.   Photograph by Arnaud Meyer.

Eshliman, was appointed in his stead; on his return, he was at long last admitted in 1837 to full membership of the Academy of Arts. He subsequently worked on the restoration of the Winter Palace after it had been gutted by the great fire of 1838, visible from eighty kilometres away, resulting from the wooden walls and floors behind the grand stone façades. At some date thereafter, he retired and went to live in Paris, where he died on 4 November 1867, aged 83, and was buried in the Père Lachaise cemetery under a rather splendid tomb, with a carved bust of his whiskery self atop, joined there in 1906 by his unmarried daughter Tatiana, born St Petersburg in 1843, died at Nice. Flowers are still laid on his well-kept grave:[1] by whom, I have been unable to discover.

[1]   Information from M. Jacques Ibry, Paris.

XI: LOOSE ENDS AT ALUPKA

Although the palace had by no means assumed its final form – the library and the billiard-room had still to be built; the pavilions were still on the roof; the lion staircase and terracing had still to be laid out – yet the apogee of Alupka's success must certainly have been the visit of the Imperial Family in September 1837, when the Tsar Nicholas I, the Tsarina, and their entourage stayed in the Palace for several days. Safontsev says that, "in addition, up to 500 persons" accompanied the royal suite, and were accommodated at Alupka:[1] this seems barely credible, for certainly the palace and its outbuildings could not accommodate so many; and the village of Alupka had then, as now, only around five hundred inhabitants.

After dinner on the first night, there were elaborate illuminations, with coloured lights hung in the trees, from the rocks, and high up the mountainside of Ai Petri; "music played unceasingly ... in some places there was a sudden spurt of flame from Bengal lights which covered the adjacent area with bright blue light ... nowhere was this spectacle so magnificent as by the lake".[2] The Empress usually passed the evening in the blue drawing-room, then furnished in the oriental style and known as the 'Seraskier Room' after the home of one Seraskier Pasha in Constantinople. The men played whist. "Sometimes Mme Bashmakova and Countess Choiseul would sing. Meanwhile a band played out of doors near the house".[3] On the following evening, as a surprise, amateur dramatics were laid on in the dining-room – *Jocrisse, ou le chef des brigands* – with a copse of real oak trees on stage, to represent a dense and impassable forest. "Music was supplied by Countess Vorontsov who played the piano ... Her Imperial Majesty was extremely pleased with it. The Grand Princess laughed heartily, saying that she had not enjoyed herself so much for a long time".[4]

On the last morning of their visit, on 29 September, a lunch on the lawn, under a trellis of vines, was given for the Tatar women of Alupka and their children. "Some of them conversed with the Empress through an interpreter and finally, after a mullah had read a prayer to Allah to preserve the health of

---

[1]   Safontsev, Visit, 1840, reprinted in *Alupka 150th Anniversary Discourses*, 2000, pp. 122–7.

[2]   *Ibid.*, pp. 122–7.

[3]   *Ibid.*

[4]   *Ibid.*

the Padishah's consort, wished the Empress a safe journey and themselves the happiness of seeing her bright eyes again soon".[1]

There were to be other visits from royalty. Captain Spencer reported in 1854 on another visit, that "a Russian officer galloped madly up to the windows of the castle, waving his hand and exclaiming 'The Tzar! The Tzar!' when a droshky, covered with dust, dashed up the avenue with the speed of lightning and the Autocrat of all the Russias was standing in the midst of us ... He spoke of England and the English in the most flattering manner; said how pleased he was to see them at all times in Russia, and hoped that, on our return, we would tell them of the beautiful scenery of the Crimea, in order that they might come in numbers and make it their summer tour".[2]

But not all visitors to Alupka were equally enchanted; perhaps tastes were beginning to change; for in 1842, another foreign visitor, J. G. Kohl, wrote: "... a castle renowned far and wide for its architectural and Hesperian splendours. The mere designs for this building and the gardens made by architects sent for expressly from London, are said to have cost 60,000 rubles. The whole is not expected to be completed under seven millions ... After these stories of the enormous sums expended on it, we were rather disappointed in the castle and park of Alupka. It is built in the Gothic style, with marble found in the vicinity, of a greenish cast, so that it does not rise well out of the landscape. The large windows do not accord with its Gothic character any more than the immensely spacious and lofty apartments. The dining-room is, indeed, magnificent – a banquetting hall fit for kings and heroes; but the books, pictures, &c., are by no means remarkable. The greatest fault, however, is undoubtedly the situation, with a mountain 4000 feet high immediately behind it, and no prospect in front but the gray desolate sea, for the four or five hundred feet of garden between are placed on a steep declivity, of which nothing can be seen from the windows but the tops of the trees".[3]

By 1844, Count Vorontsov had laboured for twenty years as Governor-General of New Russia, far longer than a usual term; "now sixty-two, practically blind from a progressive eye disorder, he was feeling generally worn out from his two decades of efforts";[4] and was much looking forward to his retirement, as a kind of English country nobleman, on his estate at Alupka now substantially, though not absolutely, completed. But in November of that year, a royal courier with a personal message from the Tsar reached him at his town house in Odessa, requesting him to "take command of all Caucasian forces and to act as the Emperor's all-powerful Caucasian Viceroy"; and suggesting that "it

[1]   Ibid.
[2]   Spencer, Turkey, Russia, the Black Sea and Circassia, 1854, pp. 282–3.
[3]   Kohl, Russia, 1842, pp. 463–4.
[4]   Rhinelander, op. cit., p. 123.

ought to take Vorontsov only about three years to put things straight. Vorontsov was frankly appalled".[1] Yet it was impossible to refuse. The blow was somewhat softened by Vorontsov's promotion from Count to Prince in the same year.

The best account of daily life at Alupka during the Prince's last years, at any rate in English, is that recorded by Lady Sheil. In the autumn of 1849, she and her husband, Sir Justin Sheil, KCB, the ambassador to the court of the Shah, were travelling overland to Persia by way of Poland and the Black Sea. In Odessa, they were introduced to the Vorontsovs, who invited them to spend a day with them at Alupka. "The sight of this gorgeous mansion struck us with surprise ... The Oriental Hall, as it is designated, is devoted to the morning reception of the numerous company".[2] Their hosts devoted the entire day to showing them all over the estate, "an operation of no small fatigue from its extent, and from its being, not hill and dale, but all hill and no dale". They found everything in perfect order, thanks to the Prince's English manager and bailiff, and noted that he also had an English librarian. That evening, there were at least fifty guests for dinner, "a number stated to be unusually small ... The wines were numerous and excellent, all supplied from the Prince's own estate".[3]

On his transfer to the Caucasus, Vorontsov was obliged to move to Tiflis, and there to take charge of never-ending warfare. The boundaries with Persia and, to a lesser extent, Turkey, had been defined twenty years earlier by, amongst others, the playwright-diplomat Griboyedov, who was murdered by a maddened Muslim mob in Teheran in 1829.[4] But the Muslim mountaineers of Daghestan and Chechnya bitterly resented the Russian incursion into their difficult terrain, and remained then (as now) unpacified. Vorontsov was not a particularly skilful general; but he was a very good administrator. "Instead of confronting the rebels with force, Vorontsov used diplomacy, including economic enticements, to drive a wedge between the rebel leaders and more and more of their supporting highland population".[5] But it was a weary, thankless, perilous and long-drawn-out task, which allowed him only occasional fleeting visits to his beloved Alupka: fortunately his wife kept the palace and park in good order, and indeed made some improvements of her own.

He was obliged to remain in Tiflis, not for three, but for ten years. Repeated requests for leave to retire were refused by the Tsar, until February, 1855, soon after the start of the Crimean War (which involved a Russo-Turkish front in the Caucasus too, a fact now mostly forgotten). In March, he travelled

[1]   *Ibid.*
[2]   Sheil, *Glimpses*, 1856, pp. 29, 30.
[3]   *Ibid.*, p. 31.
[4]   Kelly, *Diplomacy and Murder*, 2002, *passim.*
[5]   Rhinelander, *op. cit.*, p. 149.

to St Petersburg, then to Dresden, where he had a family reunion with his sister, the Countess of Pembroke (whose son, Sydney Herbert, was British Secretary of State for War, which caused embarassment on both sides); then to Carlsbad to take the waters; then back to St Petersburg. In August 1856, he attended the coronation of the Tsar Alexander II in Moscow, and received his field-marshal's baton; then home to Odessa, where he died of a stroke on 6th November 1856. All this arduous travelling cannot have helped, for despite his pleading twenty years earlier, Russia still lacked a railway network – greatly to its disadvantage during the Crimean War – and most of the many hundreds of miles he covered in his seventies, over mainly very bad roads, had to be in the family coach, or else by river. Only the lines from St Petersburg to Tsarskoe Selo, and from Moscow to St Petersburg, had been opened at this date.

After Vorontsov's death, his widow Elizaveta preferred the social life of Odessa to the comparative seclusion of Alupka; she died at a great age in 1881. The Palace, or at least part of it – now known as the Shuvalov wing – was occupied by their daughter Sofiya, her husband, and children; in 1844 she had married Count Andrey Shuvalov, a fellow-officer of Lermontov in the Imperial cavalry. The entailed estate of palace and park passed in 1856 to Prince Simon Vorontsov, who "did not distinguish himself with any talents, and in no way resembled his parent".[1] He had married in 1851 the former Princess Trubetskaya, a former maid of honour to the Empress and widow of A. G. Stolypin. "A big, large-eyed, dark-browed beauty, she was an example of the type of an aristocratic woman of the world, in whom the European foppishness was combined with the truly Russian haughtiness".[2] Perhaps unsurprisingly, the new generation found the cost of the upkeep of Alupka intolerable, cut back greatly on the hospitality of the establishment, and seldom went there. They were absent when the Prince and Princess of Wales paid a visit in April 1869, planting two trees, still standing. "About 3.30 the party sat down to a hot lunch in the noble dining-saloon of the palace, the honours being done by Prince Troubetskoy in the absence of Prince Woronzow".[3]

On the death of Prince Simon Vorontsov, childless, in 1882, his widow went to live in Italy, taking with her as much as she could manage of the palace's contents and furnishings: she lived on, abroad, until 1895, leaving a copious legacy of family litigation behind her. The palace lay largely empty for some ten years, except for occasional charity concerts and such-like, as when Chaliapin sang and Rachmaninov played there in 1898. It had passed to Count Pavel Shuvalov, son of Prince Mikhail Vorontsov's daughter, Sofiya; to whom the title also passed. On his death in 1885 his brother Mikhail inherited: he died

---

[1]   Filatova, *Vorontsov Family Portraits*, 1997 (pages un-numbered).
[2]   *Ibid.*
[3]   *The Times*, 29 April, 1869, p. 10.

in 1904, and everything then passed to their sister Elizaveta Vorontsova-Dashkova. Prince Vorontsov's grand-daughter had managed to buy back much that had been removed to Italy: and lived on here, in much reduced splendour, until the death of her husband Illarion in 1917, when his widow went to France, where she died in 1923.

Already, by 1903, "the countryside and plots of land in the vicinity of the princely park have been very much built over, as the district has become a very populous, noisy and expensive visitors' resort with hotels, furnished rooms, etc.".[1]

Disobligingly, Karl Baedeker described it in 1914 just as "The Chateau (interior uninteresting; closed 12–2)",[2] though he was somewhat kinder about the park. In 1905 the house was used as a hospital for officers after the Russo-Japanese war, since Illarion Vorontsov-Dashkov was then head of the Russian Red Cross; and again as a military hospital in 1914. It was fortunate to escape any serious damage during the Revolution and the ensuing civil war; in 1921 it became a museum, and was well looked after until the German occupation of the Crimea, when it was used for the rest and recreation of German officers: during which period, a large number of books, and no fewer than 537 paintings, disappeared. Some, but not all, have been recovered. The palace was saved from German demolition in the course of their retreat by the Crimean partisans, and at the end of the war became, once again, a museum. Winston Churchill and his entourage stayed here in February, 1945, for the Yalta Conference; they found it in mid-winter cold, draughty, and uncomfortable, but Churchill took a great fancy to Bonanni's marble lions on the terrace, one of which he thought resembled him, and asked Stalin to let him take them home: which request Stalin, not unreasonably, refused. It is thought that this may have been the only occasion when fires were lit in Blore's chimney-pieces. In his diaries, Field Marshall Lord Alanbrooke writes, "we are lodged in one of the large Crimean houses of the Tsarist nobility days. Built by a Scottish architect in semi-Moorish, semi-Scotch style! The mixture is somewhat startling". Disconcertingly, and somewhat unconvincingly, he adds "This house was occupied by the German commander of the Crimean forces, and he had been promised the house as a gift after the war. He was consequently loath to carry out any destructions similar to those on other houses till the very last moment, and finally left it too late".[3]

From 1953 to 1956 the museum was closed, most of its contents were dispersed, and it became a state dacha, an unaccountable decision: reversed in the latter year. Since then, its devoted administrators and curators have managed

---

[1] *Bol'shaya Entsiklopediya*, 1903, p. 404.
[2] Baedeker, *Russia*, 1814, p. 421.
[3] Alanbrooke, *War Diaries*, 2001, pp. 654–5.

89. The Southern Façade, Alupka: the Iwan, the verandas, the stone and ironwork balustrades, the lion stair greenery and, as ever, brooding in the background, the crags of Ai-Petri.

Photograph: Paul Barker, Country Life.

to reassemble a very respectable collection, attracting some 300,000 visitors a year. A recent threat by the Ukrainian President to turn it again into an official dacha has been successfully resisted by the local, semi-autonomous, Crimean Parliament. It remains one of the grandest architectural monuments, and tourist attractions, of the Black Sea.

XII: CONCLUSION

In October, 1853, the Ottoman Empire declared war on Russia. In November, Britain and France concluded an offensive and defensive alliance. The vast size of the Russian Empire; its enormous armies; its apparent designs on Istanbul and the Bosphorus; its steady expansion in Central Asia; and an increasing distrust of its autocratic political structure, led to deep uneasiness in the West. In January of 1854, a British fleet entered the Black Sea. France and Britain declared war on Russia on 28 March 1854. The first months of the war saw Russian victories in the Balkans, the Caucasus, and on the Black Sea. Then, in September, 1854, the Allies landed at Eupatoria. There followed the battles of Balaklava and Inkerman, which were by no means Russian defeats. But in September, 1855, Sevastopol fell to the long-drawn-out allied siege, after massive casualties on both sides. "Poor strategy, antiquated weapons, out-moded tactics, wretched supply systems and widespread incompetence would exact a terrible toll from Nicholas's armies in the Crimea as they faced the technologically superior forces of the Western Allies".[1] Not that the Allies were much more efficient: it was a near thing. But an armistice was agreed in February, and Russia finally capitulated on 30th March, 1856, by the Peace of Paris.

The Tsar Nicholas I had died, somewhat unexpectedly, early in the morning of 18 February 1855, to be succeeded by the Tsar Alexander II, whose coronation in Moscow on 26 August 1855 was dutifully attended by the aged Prince Vorontsov. On 6 November, Prince Vorontsov himself died at his palace in Odessa. It was the end of an era: the death of Nicholas I, the death of Vorontsov, and the defeat of Russia, brought to an end the period of Anglo-Russian amity. So far as I know, no English architect was thereafter invited to work in Russia.

* * * * *

It would be misleading to suggest that the English style in architecture had a predominant influence in the early nineteenth-century development of the Crimea. But against that, it most certainly cannot be ruled out altogether. Professor Shvidkovsky has argued, persuasively, that the English influence in Russia, in this period, was considerably greater than the French, Italian or

---

[1] Lincoln, *Nicholas I*, 1978, p. 316.

German influence; and not only in the field of Classical (or Neo-Classical) architecture. For the Russians in general were deeply attached to their own medieval traditions; and found they had more in common with the English Tudor or Neo-Gothic styles than with those of any other country. In the 1820s, this was true, in rather different ways, in St Petersburg; in Moscow; and in the country estates of noblemen.

Whilst this may have been only partly true of the Crimea, whose development came later than that of northern Russia, and where so much of the evidence has disappeared, Shvidkovsky says "The development of Russian neo-Gothic in the classical period came to a climax in one of the most splendid ensembles of southern Russia, Count Vorontsov's palace at Alupka on the Crimean coast, built in 1832 [sic] by Edward Blore ... one side of the palace displayed an authentic British medieval architecture, while the other struck a no less convincing Moorish note. This deliberate transformation of authentic architectural styles signalled the onset of the new century and a new era. The Enlightenment had finally made way for romanticism ...".[1]

It is said that successive Tsars felt their pre-eminence to be somewhat threatened by the grandeur of Count Vorontsov's creation. The Count, himself, was slightly horrified, in retrospect, at his own extravagance. There is a story (of somewhat uncertain authenticity) that, after its completion, Vorontsov called for all the bills and receipts, which filled several leather trunks. They were placed in his study, where, behind locked doors, he went through them all. "No one ever knew the exact amount they represented. Every bill was paid – but the Count burned all the papers and receipts which told of his outlay".[2]

Alupka is, certainly, a very grand house indeed; though by no means in the same league as great royal palaces such as Versailles or the Escorial, it can be considered in much the same light as great noblemen's houses such as Castle Howard or Vaux-le-Vicomte, though in a style more reminiscent of Abbotsford or Balmoral, except for the Oriental façade to seaward. That, however, is, like Nash's Brighton Pavilion, a one-off design, quite *sui generis*. Although Blore, in quite a short working life as an architect of little over twenty years (he retired in 1849) carried out an enormous volume of country-house work, much of it is unoriginal and pretty unimaginative. That can certainly not be said of Alupka, which seems to me to be the dazzling peak of his career.

Bakhchisaray is to some extent a Tatar version, on a more modest scale, of the Topkapi palace in Istanbul, but is nonetheless likewise *sui generis*. We are exceptionally fortunate that these two very splendid buildings should have survived almost all the vicissitudes of history. It is a great pity that so few of the other palaces and mansions of the Crimea have survived equally unaltered and

---

[1]   Shvidkovsky, *op. cit.*, 1996, p. 223.
[2]   Blanche, *Sabres of Paradise*, 1960, p. 229; Rhinelander, *op. cit.*, 1990, p. 119.

intact. In my judgement – and I have been a rank-and-file member for many years both of ICOMOS and of Europa Nostra, so I know something of the relevant criteria – Alupka and its park are worthy of the protection accorded by inscription by UNESCO on its list of World Heritage Sites. It would be good to think that the appropriate steps could be set in motion, soon, by the appropriate authorities.

90. Alupka: one of the corner towers, with pinnacles and chimneys, and flowers.
Photograph: Paul Barker, Country Life.

BIBLIOGRAPHY

Alexander, J. T., *Catherine the Great: Life and Legend*, New York and London, 1989.

Allen, Brian and Dukelskaya, Larissa (eds), *British Art Treasures from Russian Imperial Collections in the Hermitage*, New Haven & London, 1996.

Anderson, Ian G., *Scotsmen in the Service of the Czars*, Edinburgh, 1990.

Annual Register, London, 1786.

Anon., *Alupka – Chteniya po sluchayu 150–oi godovschiny [150th Anniversary Discourses]*, Simferopol, 2000.

Anon., 'Alupka, the Residence of Prince Woronzow', in *The Builder*, July 1850, VIII.

Anon., 'The Prince and Princess of Wales in the Crimea,' *The Times*, 29 April 1869.

Baedeker, Karl, *Russia*, London, 1914.

Bennigsen, A. and Wimbush, S. E., *Muslims of the Soviet Empire: A Guide*, London, 1985.

Binyon, T. J., *Pushkin*, London, 2002.

Blanche, L., *Sabres of Paradise*, London, 1960.

Bol'shaya Entsiklopediya, Moscow, 1903.

Brett, C. E. B., 'Alupka Palace, Crimea', in *Country Life*, 25 July 2002, CXCVI (30), 74–79.

Brett, C. E. B., 'Letter from Alupka', in *Times Literary Supplement*, 2 November 2001 (5144), 19.

Brett, C. E. B., 'Crimea's Garden Palace', in *Country Life*, 6 February 2003, CXCVII (6), 68–71.

Brooke, A. F. [Viscount Alanbrooke], *War Diaries*, London, 2001.

Brumfield, W. C., *A History of Russian Architecture*, Cambridge, 2003.

Cockerell, C. R., Diary, unpublished manuscript in RIBA library, London.

Colvin, H., *A Biographical Dictionary of British Architects 1600–1840*, 3rd edn, London, 1995.

Craven, Elizabeth, *Journey through the Crimea to Constantinople, 1789*, 2nd edn, Vienna, 1814.

Crook, J. Mordaunt, 'Xanadu by the Black Sea, the Woronzow Palace at Aloupka', in *Country Life*, 2 March, 1972, CLI (3899), 513–17.

Cross, A. G., *By the Banks of the Neva*, Cambridge, 1997.

Cross, A. G., *By the Banks of the Thames*, Newtonville, Mass., 1980.

Cross, A. G., 'Charles Cameron's Scottish workmen', in *Scottish Slavonic Review*, X, Spring 1988.

Demidov, A. N., *Puteshestvie v yuzhnuyu Rossiyu i Krym, sovershennoe v 1837 [Journey to Southern Russia ... in 1837]*, Moscow, 1853.

Deutschbaltisches Biographisches Lexicon, 1710–1960, Vienna, 1970.

BIBLIOGRAPHY

Dictionary of National Biography, ed. by Sir Leslie Stephen [and others], 79 vols, London, 1885–1996.

Duberly, Mrs Henry, *Journal kept during the Russian War*, London, 1855.

Edinburgh Evening Courant, Edinburgh, 1784.

Encyclopaedia Britannica, 11th edn, 29 vols, London, 1910–11.

Ernst, N. L., 'Bakhchisarai khanskii dvorets i architektor Velikogo knyazya Ivana III fryazin Aleviz Novyi' ['The Khans' Palace at Bakhchisaray and Grand Prince Ivan III's architect, the Westerner Alevisio the Younger ("Novi")], in *Zhurnal tavricheskogo obshchestva istorii, arkheologii i etnografii*, Simferopol, 1928, No. 2.

Fadeyeva, T. M., and Sokolova, M. V., *Bakhchisaray i okrestnost, [Bakhchisarai and the Vicinity]* Simferopol, 2000.

Figes, Orlando, *Natasha's Dance*, London, 2002.

Filatova, G. G., 'Aziatskiy pavil'on ili staryy dvorets Vorontsovykh v Alupke' [The Asiatic Pavilion or Old Palace of the Vorontsovs at Alupka], in *Vorontsovy i Angliya: Krymskie mezhdunarodnye vorontsovkie nauchnye chteniya* (Simferopol, Krymskiy arkhiv, 2002).

Filatova, G. G., *Semeinye portrety Vorontsovykh [Vorontsov Family Portraits]*, Simferopol, 1977.

Galichenko, A. A., *Alupka: dvorets i park [Alupka, Palace and Park]*, Kiev, 1992.

Galichenko, A. A. [and others], *Alupka putevotditel [Alupka, Guidebook]*, Moscow, 1997.

Gentleman's Magazine, London, 1829.

Gerngross, V., 'Bakhchisaraiskii khanski dvorets' ['The Palace of the Khans at Bakhchisarai'], in *Starye gody*, 1912 (April), pp. 3–29.

Girouard, M., *The Victorian Country House*, London, 1979.

[Harrison], *The Modest Genius*, Catalogue of Harrison Exhibition, Chester, 1977.

Hartley, Janet M., *Alexander I*, Harlow, 1994.

Hartley, Janet M., *A Social History of the Russian Empire, 1625–1825*, Harlow, 1999.

Howard, J. and Kuznetsov, S., 'Scottish Architecture in Czarist Russia', in *History Today*, XLVI (2), February 1996, 35–41.

Hunt, T. F., *Exemplars of Tudor Architecture adapted to Modern Habitations*, London, 1830.

Kalininin, N. and Zemlyanichenko, M., *Romanovy i Krym [Romanovs in the Crimea]*, Simferopol, 2002.

Kelly, Laurence, *Diplomacy and Murder in Tehran: Alexander Griboyedov and Imperial Russia's Mission to the Shah of Persia*, London / New York, 2002.

Kohl, J. G., *Russia*, London, 1842.

Korshunova, M., 'William Hastie in Russia', in *Architectural History*, XVII, 1974, pp. 14–20.

Levey, Michael, *The World of Ottoman Art*, London, 1975.

Lillford, Ralph, 'Hogarth's The Politician', in *Apollo*, CXVII, February 1983,100.

Lincoln, W. B., *Nicholas I, Emperor and Autocrat of All the Russias*, London, 1978.

Loudon, J. C., *Encyclopaedia of Gardening*, London, 1834.

Lowe, R., *Sir Samuel Meyrick & Goodrich Court*, Herefordshire, 2003.

Madariaga, Isabel de, *Russia in the Age of Catherine the Great*, London, 1981.

Madariaga, Isabel de, *Catherine the Great: a Short History*, New Haven/London, 1990.

Mansel, Philip, *Prince of Europe: the Life of Charles Joseph de Ligne*, London, 2003.

Marmont, Maréchal (Duc de Raguse), *Voyage*, 5 volumes, Paris, 1837.

Marsh, Madeleine, 'Russian Riviera, Carlo Bossoli's Water-Colours', in *World of Interiors*, January 1989, 78–85.

Massingberd, H. M., and Sykes, C. S., *Great Houses of Ireland*, London, 1999.

Meller, H. D., *Blore's Country Houses*, unpublished MA thesis, Courtauld Institute, London, 1974.

Meller, H. D., 'From Engraver to Architect', in *Country Life*, 19 October 1978, pp. 1205–6.

Mikeshin, M. I., *Mikhail Vorontsov*, St Petersburg, 1998, not printed, available on website http://ideashistory.org.ru/books/mikesh1/english/engtitle.htm

Montefiore, Simon Sebag, *Prince of Princes: the Life of Potemkin*, London, 2000.

Ockrim, M. A. R., *The Life and Works of Thomas Harrison of Chester*, unpublished Ph D thesis, Courtauld Institute, London, 1988.

Palchikova, A. P., 'F. F. El'son, Pervyi arkhitektor yuzhnogo berega Kryma' [F. F. Elson, Principal Architect of the South Coast of the Crimea, in *Kul'tura narodov prichrmomor'ya*, No 2, Simferopol, December 1997, pp. 185–9.

Parkinson, John, *A Tour of Russia, Siberia and the Crimea 1792–1794*, London, 1971, 193–8.

Porter, R. K., *Travelling Sketches in Russia and Sweden during the years 1805–1808*, London, 1809.

Portoghesi, P., *Dizionario Enciclopedico di Architettura e Urbanistica*, Rome, 1968.

Rae, Isobel, *Charles Cameron, Architect to the Court of Russia*, London, 1971.

Raguse, Duc de (Maréchal Marmont), *Voyage*, 5 volumes, Paris, 1837.

Reeves-Smyth, T., *Crom Castle Demesne*, 2 volumes, 1982, National Trust (unpublished).

Reeves-Smyth, T., 'An Elizabethan Revival House in Ireland: Edward Blore and the Building of Crom, Co Fermanagh', in Reeves-Smyth, T. and Oram, R. (eds), *Avenues to the Past*, Belfast, 2003, pp. 321–52.

Reeves-Smyth, T. and Oram, R. (eds), *Avenues to the Past*, Belfast, 2003.

Rhinelander, A. L. H., *Prince Michael Vorontsov, Viceroy to the Tsar*, Montreal, 1990.

Rowan, A., *North West Ulster*, London, 1979.

Safontsev, S. V., '*Opisanie prebyvaniya Imperatorskoi familii v Krymu v sentyabre 1837 goda [Description of the Imperial Family's Visit to the Crimea in September 1837]*, Odessa, 1840.

Serbov, N., in *Russian Biographical Dictionary* (reprint 1962), vol xxiv.

Seymour, H. D., *Russia on the Black Sea and Sea of Azof*, London, 1855.

Sheil, Mary, *Glimpses of Life and Manners in Persia*, London, 1856.

Shiryaev, S. D., *Alupka, dvorets i park: putevoditel' [Alupka, Palace and Park: Guidebook]*, Simferopol, 1927.

Shiryaev, S. D., 'Usadebnaya arkhitektura Kryma v 1820–1840 gg.' ['Estate Architecture in the Crimea, 1820–1840'], in *Krym*, VIII, 1928, pp. 72–102.

Shvidkovsky, D., *The Empress and the Architect*, New Haven and London, 1996.

Shvidkovsky, D., 'The Empress and the Architect', in *Country Life*, 16 November 1988, CLXXXIII (46), 90–5.

BIBLIOGRAPHY

Skelton, Joseph, *Antient Armour from the Collection at Goodrich Court, Herefordshire*, 2 vols, Oxford / London, 1833.

Skempton, A. W., and others (eds), *Biographical Dictionary of Civil Engineers in Great Britain and Ireland, 1: 1500–1830*, London, 2002.

Spencer, Captain, *Turkey, Russia, the Black Sea and Circassia*, London, 1854.

Timofeev, L. M., 'K voprosu o genezise kompozitsii vorontsovskoga dvortsa v Alupka' [The origins of the composition of the Vorontsov Palace at Alupka], in *Istoriya i teoriya arkhitektury i gradostroitel'stva*, Leningrad, 1980, pp. 150–4.

Vlasiuk, A., 'O rabote zodchego Alevizia Novogo v Bakhchisarae i v Moskovskom Kremle [The works of Alevisio Novi at Bakhchisaray and in the Kremlin at Moscow], in *Arkhitekturnoe nasledstvo*, 10, 1958, pp. 101–10.

Voltaire, F. M. A. de, *Correspondence*, ed. Besterman.

Vorontsov, M., 'Autobiographical Notes, 1803–1833', unpublished manuscript, D 3044/C/1,2 in Public Record Office of Northern Ireland.

Wilmot, Martha and Catherine, *Russian Journals 1803–1808*, London, 1934.

Wright, L., *Clean and Decent*, 2nd edn, London, 2000, *passim*.

91. The author, on the roof of the Alupka Palace.
Photograph by Terence Reeves-Smyth.

· ПЛАНЫ · И · ФАСАДАМЫ ·

· БЫВШАГО ·

· ХАНСКАГО · ДВОРЦА ·

· ВЪ ·

· БАКЧИСАРАЙ ·

· СЪ · РАЗНЫМЪ · СТРОЕНIЯМЪ ·

· ВЪ ·

КРИМУ

· М · DCC · XCVIII · ГОДА ·